Diverse Methods for Research and Assessment of College Students

Edited by

Frances K. Stage

American Counseling Association
5999 Stevenson Avenue
Alexandria, VA 22304

Cover Concept by Christopher Stage
Cover Design by Kay Bollen

Library of Congress Cataloging-in-Publication Data

Diverse methods for research and assessment of college students /
    edited by Frances K. Stage.
        p. cm.
    Includes bibliographical references.
    ISBN 1-55620-096-X
    1. College students—United States—Rating of. 2. Research—
Methodology. I. Stage, Frances K.
LA229.D56 1992
378.1'98'072073—dc20   92-9505
                                                                           CIP

Printed in the United States of America

Dedication

The semester before Egon Guba retired, I was privileged, as a new assistant professor, to "sit in" on his Educational Inquiry course. That experience taught me more about myself and my beliefs as a researcher than any experience before or since. Six of the eight authors in this volume were fortunate to have had that experience. This book is dedicated to Egon Guba who changed the meaning of educational research through his tireless efforts—but always with a sense of humor. It is hoped that this book, in a small way, carries forward his work.

Table of Contents

Contributors

Frances K. Stage is associate professor of higher education and student affairs at Indiana University, Bloomington. She earned BS and MS degrees in mathematics. Her PhD is in higher education from Arizona State University. She has extensive experience working with college students and has published book chapters, guest editorials, and articles focusing on college students and techniques for studying them. She is a coauthor of *New Directions for Student Services: Framework for Creating a Multicultural Campus Environment* and currently serves on the editorial boards of the *Journal of College Student Development* and the *Review of Higher Education*.

Louis C. Attinasi, Jr., is assistant professor of higher education at the University of Houston. He uses ethnographic research techniques in his studies of college student persistence. His writing focuses particularly on diverse college students.

Jill Ellen Carnaghi is director of residence life at the University of Vermont. For 10 years she held progressively more responsible positions in residence hall systems in the East, Midwest, and West and was assistant to the dean of the School of Education at Indiana University. She has worked closely with students in achieving cooperative, developmental living environments. Her scholarly writing and research interests include leadership, educational programming, and interpersonal development.

Kathleen Manning is assistant professor of higher education and student affairs at the University of Vermont. She has served as assistant dean of students at Emerson College, director of student activities at Curry College, and executive assistant to the dean of student life at Trenton State College. Her research and scholarly writing include campus cultures, organizational development, multiculturalism, and qualitative research methodology applied to higher education. She is a coauthor of *New Directions for Student Services: Framework for Creating a Multicultural Campus Environment.*

Amaury Nora is assistant professor of higher education at the University of Illinois-Chicago. He has conducted numerous studies of college student satisfaction and persistence. His research focuses on diverse students on the college campus and community college students.

Ruth V. Russell is associate professor and assistant department chair of recreation and park administration at Indiana University. She also has extensive teaching and administrative experience at West Virginia University. She won numerous awards for excellence in undergraduate teaching and founded an international institute and refereed journal on higher education in recreation and leisure studies. She is the author of *Leadership in Recreation* and *Planning Programs in Recreation.* Her research and scholarly writing include student learning and classroom pedagogy, leisure and life satisfaction, and research methods.

Robert A. Schwartz is assistant professor of educational leadership and policies at the University of South Carolina, Columbia. He has over 10 years' experience in career planning and placement and counseling and upper level student affairs administration. He has worked extensively with Greek organizations. His research and scholarly writing include Greek affairs, alcohol abuse, and the history of the student affairs profession.

Elizabeth J. Whitt is assistant professor of higher education at Iowa State University. She previously was assistant professor at Oklahoma State University. She has worked in residence life and student affairs administration, including 4 years as dean of students at Doane College. Her research and scholarly writing include high quality out-of-class experiences for undergraduates, faculty socialization, qualitative research methods in exploring institutional cultures, and team approaches to qualitative research.

Foreword

Over the past several decades much of the research on college and university students has been concerned to a significant degree with trying to describe the experiences of students in a quantitative sense. Although there are several notable exceptions, a review of the titles listed in Pascarella and Terenzini's 1991 landmark publication, *How College Affects Students*, leads to the inescapable conclusion that research has been conducted to great extent through the use of quantitative research methodology.

Pascarella and Terenzini observed that "The positivistic, quantitative paradigm has served us well. The vast preponderance of what we know about the impact of college has been learned from this approach to inquiry" (p. 632). But they assert that much more work needs to be done about the college student experience: ". . . there is still much important fine-grained work to be done" (p. 632). I agree. At this juncture in the study of college students, assessment methods in addition to the commonly used quantitative techniques can be extremely valuable. Thus this publication is particularly timely and will help student affairs officers, faculty, and others enhance their skills in conducting alternative forms of assessment. I wish this publication had been available 3 years ago when I began my own research using forms of assessment techniques other than the quantitative approaches I had learned in graduate school. Rather than relying on the then extant literature on qualitative research, much of which was directed at conducting research from an anthropological or sociological perspective, by studying this publication I would have been able to conduct my work with greater precision on a more timely basis.

A great deal can be learned about college and university students using methods other than the traditional survey instrument. Several years ago Jim Lyons, then the chief student affairs officer at Stanford University, suggested to me that by asking students the question, "If you were in charge of your university for a day, what would be the one thing you would not change?'' you can find out what is most valuable from the student perspective about the college. Peggy Barr, the vice chancellor for student affairs at Texas Christian University, frequently has made the persuasive case that enormous amounts of information about students reside in the records that institutions keep on every student.

Information about students abounds on every campus. If you want to know about the incidence of sexually transmitted diseases on your campus, the student health service has the information in aggregate form. Are there increasing occurrences of hate behavior on campus? Your physical plant staff can tell you all about the graffiti they eradicate from rest rooms, bulletin boards, and out-of-the-way walls. Is destructive behavior related to alcohol and other drugs on the rise? The campus police department will have records that speak to this question. What are the burning issues on campus? Read the letters to the editor of the student newspaper over a period of time to get a sense of what is on the minds of students. These issues, and countless others, can be addressed through the research methods described in this publication.

Much of what is discussed here will be helpful in determining the answer to the question "Why?" Quantitative methods do not lend themselves easily to explanations about why students do what they do or what they recommend to improve the quality of campus life. In a focus group, asking students about, for example, why they chose to enroll in the university, why they elected to stay at the university, and why they chose their major will yield thick, rich data that will help us better understand them. In the College Experiences Study, of which I was co-principal investigator, we interviewed over 1,300 people, reviewed countless file drawers of documents, and spent many hours observing students in our attempt to identify the institutional factors and conditions that make for a high-quality student experience. This kind of study would not have been possible had we been unable to discuss issues in detail with students, faculty, administrators, and others for prolonged periods of time. In some cases we interviewed people more than once to make sure that we understood their views on the topics at hand.

One of the potential misconceptions about the research methods discussed in this publication is that they are easy to apply in the field, that they are less rigorous than quantitative methods. Nothing could be farther from the truth. These methods, when applied with precision, take more time, greater resources, and certainly as much conceptual ability as quantitative measures. Making precise the meaning of language, for example, is not easy because language for the purposes of understanding college and university students cannot be reduced by use of statistical formulas. Qualitative methods require every bit as much skill as quantitative methods, so the reader should not assume that the approaches described are an easy shortcut to conducting valuable research.

The richness of this research cannot be matched, in my opinion, by quantitative methods. Indeed, as Pascarella and Terenzini pointed out, "When employed judiciously, such approaches (naturalistic and qualitative methodologies) are capable of providing greater sensitivity to many of the subtle and fine-grained complexities of college impact than the more traditional quantitative approaches" (1991, p. 634).

Because I have had a chance to review several drafts of this book, I have already utilized ideas shared by the authors for such disparate projects as developing an understanding of the benefits of membership in historically African-American fraternities and sororities, evaluating the Literacy Volunteers of America-Wichita Area reading program, and reviewing the residence hall food service from the perspective of students on my campus. These projects lent themselves very well to the methods described in this publication because in each case my colleagues and I were attempting to gain a better understanding of the human experience. I think this publication will provide excellent blueprints for how to understand the experiences of college and university students more fully than we have in the past.

Frances K. Stage in chapter 1 and Louis C. Attinasi and Amaury Nora in chapter 2 frame the issues related to alternative methods of assessment of college students. They make the case, compelling in my view, that the time to use alternative methods is now as we attempt to learn more about the experiences of college students. The second section, concerned with approaches to assessment, includes a discussion of the use of nonreactive measures in chapter 3 by Ruth V. Russell, the case study approach in chapter 4 by Kathleen Manning, and the use of historical methods in chapter 5 by Robert A. Schwartz. These chapters are full of excellent ideas about how to study college and university students. The third section is concerned with techniques, including Elizabeth J. Whitt on document analysis in chapter 6, Kathleen Manning describing ethnographic interviews in chapter 7, and Jill Ellen Carnaghi on the use of focus groups in chapter 8. Add these techniques to your evaluation repertoire. They will provide you with an exciting array of methods for collecting data. Chapter 9 by Frances K. Stage and Ruth V. Russell, and chapter 10 by Frances K. Stage conclude the book by integrating the ideas of the other authors in the book.

This publication should be read by a variety of people. Student affairs staff and department heads will find the ideas useful in evaluating their programs, experiences, and services. Chief student affairs officers will find the ideas useful as they prepare reports for their governing boards and regional accrediting agencies, or for their chief executive officers who may ask the simple but penetrating question, "What can you tell me about the experiences of the students on our campus?" College student affairs preparation program faculty, if they are not already contemporary in their knowledge of these research techniques, should read this publication and integrate these ideas in the courses they offer to graduate students. And graduate students ought to read this publication because the kinds of techniques described in it represent, in my opinion, the vanguard of assessment approaches as we move to a new century.

In the final analysis, the argument that one type of method is superior to another misses the point. Quantitative and qualitative methodologies have strengths and weaknesses. My position is that aspects of each approach can be applied to the assessment setting depending on the objectives of the project. Evaluators will be more effective if they have a wide variety of skills and techniques that they can utilize depending on the exigencies of the specific study they wish to undertake. Familiarity with the material in this publication will facilitate the development of a more robust portfolio of evaluation strategies.

We in student affairs are obliged to the chapter authors and editor of this publication for assembling these excellent ideas. They have done a splendid job. Next time you want to learn more about the experiences of college and university students, use the techniques described in this publication as a guide. You will not be disappointed with the results!

John H. Schuh
Associate Vice President
for Student Affairs
Wichita State University
Wichita, Kansas

REFERENCE

Pascarella, E. T., & Terenzini, P. T. (1991). *How college affects students.* San Francisco: Jossey-Bass.

Preface

This book grew out of discussions at the 1990 meeting of the American College Personnel Association (ACPA) in St. Louis. There, at several meetings, I heard faculty, administrators, and editors talk about problems with the new ways of conducting research and assessment. Although many were well versed in the elements of a good research design for a traditional study, many were unsure of what to look for when evaluating other approaches. Still others wanted to incorporate more diverse techniques in their own repertoires of information gathering. I consulted with John Schuh, then editor of ACPA Media, about the need for a publication on a variety of methods. I am grateful to John, who, together with Ruth Russell and Kathleen Manning, provided suggestions for chapters that might be included. This publication is the final product of those discussions.

The purpose of this publication is to provide an introduction to a variety of alternate approaches and methods for assessing and researching the college student experience, and it can serve as a resource for all those interested in the topic of research and assessment. It is intended to be useful to the administrator who seeks new information on college and university students, to those who are "consumers" of assessment and research reports, and to those who seek to increase the applicability of their own research.

Although practical limitations do not allow us to create a compendium of all possible approaches and techniques (as if such a comprehensive list could be generated and agreed to by all the editors and reviewers), we hope that presenting a selected few of the myriad alternatives will inspire change. We seek to provide introductions to approaches and techniques that will be most accessible and useful to those working with college students. We hope to motivate readers to explore some of these and other techniques in more detail and to begin to incorporate them into their own work on campus. By employing some of the approaches and techniques suggested in this publication, researchers, project directors, and campus assessors may begin to paint more complete and more useful pictures of their campus environments.

Throughout the publication, we keep in mind those in the "trenches" of student affairs work: those persons asking questions that require immediate answers and those persons with longer term research goals. We view our audience as ranging from students in a master's program just beginning to learn about research to upper level administrators puzzling about new ways to find answers to old questions. Within the publication, we talk to researchers as well as assessment officers.

The term *research* as used throughout this publication is meant to include assessment as well as the more traditional meanings of the word. The techniques discussed can be used for any kind of research on college and university students. They will be helpful for those who conduct "action-oriented" research such as assessment as well as those who conduct "pure" research that is not necessarily directly applicable. We all can benefit from recognizing new validities in others' research—and invalidities in our own.

Currently, there are no other works that deal with diverse methods specifically as they relate to the study and assessment of college students. There are in-depth books on individual assessment and research methods (e.g., Sage publications) that are referred to throughout for those who want more information on a specific topic. Readers are encouraged to identify the approach that appeals to them—that seems to address their particular questions—and expand their horizons beyond the scope of this publication.

There are four major sections in this publication: introduction, approaches, techniques, and conclusion. The first chapter of the *introduction* discusses the general need for increased flexibility in research and assessment of college and university students, and chapter 2 provides a more specific argument. We see that most of the widely employed ways of measuring or assessing college students can mask the experiences of many students on a diverse campus. Three chapters describe various general *approaches* to research and assessment of college students: nonreactive measures, the case study, and historical analysis. Three further chapters provide detailed introductions to specific research *techniques*: document analysis, the ethnographic interview, and focus groups. Each of these six chapters contains an introduction to the particular approach or method, advantages and disadvantages, and standards for conducting and reporting the results. Also included in each chapter are brief descriptions of examples of uses of the method within higher education and recommendations for further reading.

The first chapter of the *conclusion* presents a discussion of the rationale for employing a variety of methods for the study and assessment of college and university students. Examples of such combinations or triangulation are included as well as an enjoinder for all to seek multiple ways of learning about the college student on campus. The final chapter encourages us to be brave and expansive in our ideas about research. The campus of the future demands that we be willing to deviate from tried and true notions and seek answers to previously unasked questions.

Finally, I want to thank several people for providing invaluable help in the preparation of this book. Joyce Regester provided innumerable hours of assistance and advice on the manuscript, and she spent many hours assembling the manuscript and handling correspondence problems while I was in Malaysia. Graduate students John Downey and Gina Wantz deserve thanks for conducting a methods analysis of articles in the *Journal of College Student Development*. ACPA Media reviewers Stephanie Beardsley, David White, and Bob Young together with ACPA Media editor John Schuh—and then Harold Cheatham as incoming editor— provided invaluable comments on earlier versions of this book. Finally, my son Chris Stage, with assistance from siblings Bill and Katharine, made suggestions for the cover design.

chapter 1

The Case for Flexibility in Research and Assessment of College Students

Frances K. Stage

As we move toward the beginning of a new century, it is important that our visions of higher education, reflected in research and assessment of the college campus, move with us. Many of those who seek to understand and describe the campus environment present a limited vision of the world. By conditioning or by habit, they turn to the surveys, standardized instruments, and structured interviews despite an abundance of useful, creative, and eye-opening research techniques. This chapter focuses on the limitations of relying on only a few ways of collecting information, and provides a justification for learning new and creative ways to increase our knowledge of college and university students and the student experience. The chapter also provides a brief introduction to some issues of research design and basic definitions as well as suggestions for further reading.

THE LITERATURE TO DATE

Research on college and university students has been conducted extensively throughout the 20th century (Blandin, 1909; Greenleaf, 1952;

1

Minnesota University, 1924; Olin, 1909), and it has shown a remarkable evolution in terms of quantitative methodological sophistication. The earliest studies reported percentages or examined simple correlations of one factor with another (Cooper, 1928; Cummings, 1949; Iffert, 1958). Gradually authors moved to speculations about conceptual relationships and, eventually, to attempts at explanation of those relationships (Bean & Metzner, 1985; Pascarella, Ethington, & Smart, 1988; Terenzini & Wright, 1987; Tinto, 1975). Currently, some authors urge researchers to move beyond explanation of what is happening today and focus research toward attempts to influence future possibilities (e.g., Gage, 1989; Stage, 1990; Stage & Kuh, 1992). This perspective, critical theory, may be helpful to those seeking new ways to gather data on their campuses and to effect change in those environments.

Despite this evolution in the ways that quantitative data are analyzed, changes to approaches to data collection do not evolve as readily. Many of those who currently practice in the field of student affairs have only superficial knowledge of the various techniques that may be used to collect data on college and university students. Thus they understandably limit themselves in approaching data collection (typically a standardized questionnaire, locally designed survey, or structured interview) despite the benefits of using other methods. Further, because of this lack of knowledge, they may be uncomfortable reading research that employs alternative techniques.

With the development of the assessment movement in the United States has come an attendant dissatisfaction with traditional, standardized measures of student growth and development in higher education institutions (Banta, Lambert, Pike, Schmidhammer, & Schneider, 1987; Ewell, 1988; Terenzini, 1989). The earliest assessments of campus outcomes were based on research on student outcomes and persistence. Such assessments were viewed as "action research" conducted by institutional research offices (Ewell, 1988). Today, there are powerful instruments such as Pace's (1984) College Student Experiences Questionnaire (CSEQ), the ACT College Outcomes Measures Project (COMP), and the Educational Testing Service's Academic Profile based on the work of these early, campus-specific assessment efforts.

Unfortunately, the information provided by these instruments does not always completely satisfy our needs to learn about the college student experience. Fortunately, we can elicit other kinds of information easily. Administrators, researchers, and professionals need to understand the alternatives that exist for the collection of data on the college student experience. Additionally, there is a need for consumers of such information to discern high quality research and assessment.

Alternative methods of data collection are not new; Komarovsky (1953), Leon (1975), and Perry (1970) employed nonquantitative measures in their studies of college students. During the 1980s a continual discussion raged about the merits of new perspectives from which to evaluate, research, and describe (Fry, Chantavanich, & Chantavanich, 1981; Keller, 1986; Lincoln, 1986; Rist, 1977; J. K. Smith, 1983; M. L. Smith, 1986). Descriptions of these various perspectives are provided at the end of this chapter.

Despite the availability of many options for data collection, however, inflexibility reigns. Whether attempting to conduct an assessment or research, most rely solely on surveys and standardized tests even though there are limitations inherent in these particular methods of data collection. Kuh, Bean, Bradley, and Coomes (1986) analyzed articles on college students in seven journals over a 14-year period. For those researchers who collected information from students, the overwhelming method of choice was the survey. An examination of the last 5 years of the *Journal of College Student Development* (1986–1990) revealed that of those articles that described collected data, 231 out of 263, or 88%, were based on surveys or questionnaires. These survey and questionnaire methods usually require quantitative analyses and reporting of results. Only occasionally do they include reporting qualitative information as well. Articles based on only qualitative techniques are rare (Downey & Wantz, 1990).

In our efforts to talk in quantitative terms, we strip away idiosyncrasies that are important to understanding the college student experience (Parker, 1977; Stage, 1989). By stripping away those idiosyncrasies, we imply that anything that is important to know about students on our campus can be reduced to numbers. Details about students, their personal lives, and the influences on the college experience are lost. This approach produces limitations that result in gaps between those who gather information and the student affairs practitioners who use it—and who cannot ignore details about college students' lives. These limitations have been extensively discussed (Caple & Voss, 1983; Conrad, 1989; Keller, 1986; Lincoln, 1986; Strange, 1983). In ignoring or losing important information that could be gained through less traditional research techniques, our work is often not useful to administrators, educators, and policy makers.

Through the 1980s, other methods began to appear with greater frequency in the higher education and student affairs literature. Techniques for conducting research on college students became increasingly diverse. The variety of methods includes ethnographic interviews (Belenky, Clinchy, Goldberger, & Tarule, 1986; Gilligan, 1982; Milne,

1989; Tierney, 1990), the case study (Manning, 1989; Whitt, 1989), the phenomenological interview (Attinasi, 1989), and nonreactive measures (Heikinheimo & Shute, 1986). Increasingly, those who study college students have discovered that many of their most burning questions could not be answered through simple quantitative approaches to data collection and analysis.

REASONS FOR INCREASING OUR FLEXIBILITY

A recent experience serves to illustrate one of a number of invalidity problems inherent in survey methods. Like many of those whose major enterprise is collecting and interpreting data, I am inclined to respond to requests for responses to others' data collection. I ask many people to participate in my data collections; the least I can do is reciprocate. Recently however, I stopped about one-third of the way through a survey. I had already spent 30 minutes answering detailed questions and could not justify another hour to complete the task. I returned the partially completed survey knowing that it would probably not be used. I could not help wondering about what kind of sample the researcher might get—those who are incredibly persistent about completing tasks they begin or those who have a large amount of leisure time and choose to spend it filling out surveys.

Such self-selection (deciding whether or not to complete a questionnaire) is only one of the problems that comes with relying exclusively on survey data (unless one is collecting information from a captive group of students who must participate, and that brings its own set of problems). Assumptions inherent in sole reliance on surveys, structured interviews, and standardized instruments include (a) everything important to consider can be obtained through the survey (questionnaire, structured interview) format; (b) whoever constructed the instrument knows exactly what is important to ask college students; (c) students who participate in the data collection are representative, for example, of all college students in the nation, at this type of college, on this campus; (d) students are equally adept at responding to multiple choice, fill in the blank, verbal response, or open-ended survey questions; and (e) the information sought is not available elsewhere. A discussion of each assumption follows:

- *Everything important to consider can be obtained through the survey, questionnaire, or interview format.* A researcher once said, "If I can't measure it, it doesn't exist." Although few researchers display such hubris today, those who collect data from college students seem to hold this notion. The corollary for the study of college students might be "If it can't be asked on a survey, questionnaire, or quick interview, it's unimportant." Clearly, the method of choice for those seeking information about college students and their experiences has been the survey. As campus issues become more complex and students more diverse, the quick answer becomes less useful.

- *The designer of the instrument knows exactly what is important to ask about the college student experience and therefore can construct an instrument designed to ask specific questions about those things.* How many of us have conducted an interview with a student, expected to hear one thing, and ended up in a discussion that took a totally different direction? As we become more experienced as administrators, we are carried farther from the perspective of our own undergraduate days. Additionally, it is becoming increasingly likely that not all the students we seek to understand share a common background and culture. Assessment and research should be open to the possible emergence of hidden issues, new themes, and unpredicted discoveries.

- *Students who participate in this data collection are representative, for example, of all college students in the nation, at this type of college, on my campus.* There is no guarantee that the students who are accessible to those distributing an instrument or conducting an interview, and who ultimately respond, are representative. Analysis shows that if participation is voluntary, respondents are more likely to be White, female, traditional-age college students. Unless the data collection effort is compulsory, or care is taken to ensure a representative sample, the results may not reflect the sentiments of the population. Those who are most interested or enthusiastic about a topic are more likely to respond, thus giving an unbalanced view of campus life.

For example, suppose admissions office staff want information about prospective students in their geographic location for recruiting and promotional programming. A mail survey of randomly selected local high school juniors and seniors might seem like the obvious solution. However, the aim is to learn about students who are uninterested in college in general, or in the college in particular. These are precisely the students least likely to return the survey. Conducting focus groups of local high school students who are not planning to attend college or of students who have committed to other colleges and universities may produce more useful information.

- *All students are equally adept at responding to multiple choice, fill in the blank, verbal response, or open-ended survey questions.* It is widely known that there are differences in students' verbal and written skills and that some students are more adept than others at moving successfully through a standardized test battery (Powell & Steelman, 1984). An attempt to assess students' cognitive growth that relies solely on responses to a structured interview may underestimate "value added" for some students. Similarly, relying on changes in standardized instrument scores, such as using equations for intellectual growth calculated from incoming Scholastic Aptitude Test and senior year Graduate Record Exam scores, could produce exaggerated or underestimated results for students who have test anxiety. Open-ended responses may accurately reflect the opinions of many students; however, opinions of low verbal and English-as-a-second-language (ESL) students may go unreported or misinterpreted.

- *The information sought is not available elsewhere.* Given the current climate of assessment, evaluation, and data storage and retrieval on college campuses, it is possible that much of the information sought has already been collected. Additionally, in this climate of scarce resources, existing databases could be used, and important new information could be collected and analyzed through less traditional means. For example, to examine campus safety we could conduct a document analysis of campus police records and record responses of focus groups of students discussing the issue. A career development office's analysis of trends in employment since 1970 could examine historical information from office archives and conduct surveys of current students rather than conduct an expensive mail survey of alumni. Campus data systems for financial aid, registrar's records, the campus newspaper, and student activities records are also examples of the rich depositories of information waiting to be utilized.

Although not all the assumptions just discussed cause problems every time data are collected, just one or two of them can result in consistent sources of invalidity in our most widely used ways of learning about the college and university student experience. Through a wider use of qualitative approaches, we can move research and assessment of college and university students beyond the status quo and expand student affairs literature beyond what we have learned through overuse of the same traditional methods.

DEFINITIONS

Definitions helpful to readers of this publication and germane to any discussion of a variety of approaches to data collection include the following:

- *authenticity and trustworthiness*—techniques to assure the faithfulness of emergent paradigm constructions to the respondents' knowledge
- *emergent paradigm*—a view of the world that recognizes multiple realities and mutual causality and results in research that is time- and context-bound
- *naturalistic perspective*—a view that seeks to elucidate phenomena within their natural contexts
- *positivistic perspective*—a view seeking bits of knowledge as integral parts of one whole that is ultimately completely describable and controllable
- *postpositivistic perspective*—a view of the world that seeks bits of knowledge in an attempt to understand portions of an underlying reality
- *qualitative methods*—techniques employing description of the constructs of interest (such as interviewing, document analysis, observation)
- *quantitative methods*—measures requiring that a numerical or other evaluative symbol be assigned to the construct of interest
- *validity*—the extent to which a measure or observation describes what it is purported to describe.

The traditional mode of data collection in education is quasi-experimental. From this perspective, also called positivistic, researchers exert a high degree of control over the conditions of data collection as well as the questions asked, hence limiting the information collected. For example, researchers studying retention from a positivistic perspective may include only students from a highly selective university in their sample, controlling the conditions of data collection. Additionally, they may collect the information through a questionnaire, thus limiting the type and scope of information collected.

Less traditional approaches to data collection exert less control over the conditions of the data collection and/or the information collected. At the logical opposite from positivistic research designs are those conducted from the constructivist or naturalistic perspectives. Here the researcher exerts little control over conditions as well as little control over the information collected. Rather than control, the researcher seeks an understanding of the phenomenon under study from the respondent's perspective. Instead of being concerned with issues of validity, the researcher is concerned with issues of authenticity and trustworthiness. For example, researchers studying retention from the naturalistic perspective probably include a purposive sample of a small number of students and choose ethnically diverse students attending a particular institution. They conduct open-ended interviews with students to seek details of the students' lives. They may ask them to describe their lives on campus, what is important to them at college, who provides support, what presents frustration. The questions asked are open ended and free ranging. The case study or final report requires a technique that is descriptive and interpretive. No attempt is made to generalize. The reader of the report is free to learn vicariously from the detailed descriptions and interpretations of each student. For further descriptions of this perspective see Guba and Lincoln, 1981; Lincoln and Guba, 1985; and Spradley, 1979.

It should be noted that *approach to data collection* or *perspective* is not synonymous with *method* or *technique.* Using a qualitative method does not guarantee adoption of the emergent paradigm. We can be quite positivistic while conducting an interview. For example, in conducting interviews of students' moral decision making, a researcher may attend only to mentions of legal rights and ignore references to responsibility toward others. Similarly, employing a quantitative method does not mean that we are positivistic. For example, a researcher could conduct a case study of students with learning disabilities at a particular college through ethnographic interviews of 12 students; but quantifying certain information, such as noting that 9 of the 12 experienced difficulty conveying their disabilities to faculty members, does not make the research positivistic. It is in the researcher's and respondent's mutual constructions of their experience that place the study within the emergent paradigm framework.

These perspectives and ideological debates cannot be discussed fully here. The interested reader is encouraged to pursue these dilemmas through references cited throughout this chapter, in discussions with colleagues, and through attending pertinent sessions at professional meetings. It is hoped that this publication will lead to an expansion of our knowledge about the college student and result in richer and more useful information.

FURTHER READING

In addition to the references listed at the end of this chapter, readers who are interested in topics not covered here (for example, critical incidents analysis, single subject design, secondary data analysis) may want to consult publications such as Sage's Applied Social Research Methods series or Qualitative Research Methods series. Further, both the New Directions for Institutional Research and the New Directions for Research in the Behavioral and Social Sciences series contain discussions of many relevant research issues.

REFERENCES

Attinasi, L., Jr. (1989). Getting in: Mexican Americans' perceptions of university attendance and the implications for freshman year persistence. *Journal of Higher Education, 60,* 247–277.

Banta, T. W., Lambert, E. W., Pike, G. R., Schmidhammer, J. L., & Schneider, J. A. (1987, April). *Estimated score gain on the ACT COMP exam: Valid tool for institutional assessment?* Paper presented at the annual meeting of the American Educational Research Association, Washington, DC.

Bean, J. P., & Metzner, B. S. (1985). A conceptual model of nontraditional undergraduate student attrition. *Review of Educational Research, 55,* 484–540.

Belenky, M., Clinchy, B., Goldberger, N., & Tarule, J. (1986). *Women's ways of knowing: The development of self, voice, and mind.* New York: Basic Books.

Blandin, I. M. (1909). *History of higher education of women in the South prior to 1870.* New York: Neale.

Caple, R. B., & Voss, C. H. (1983). Communication between consumers and producers of student affairs research. *Journal of College Student Personnel, 24,* 38–42.

Conrad, C. F. (1989). Meditations on the ideology of inquiry in higher education: Exposition, critique, and conjecture. *Review of Higher Education, 12*(3), 199–220.

Cooper, L. B. (1928). A study in freshman elimination in one college. *Nation's Schools, 2*(3), 25–29.

Cummings, E. C. (1949). Causes of student withdrawals at DePauw University. *School & Society, 70,* 152–153.

Downey, J., & Wantz, G. (1990). *An examination of research methods employed in the Journal of College Student Development.* Unpublished manuscript.

Ewell, P. T. (1988). Outcomes, assessment, and academic improvement: In search of usable knowledge. In J. Smart (Ed.), *Higher education: Handbook of theory and research* (Vol. 5). New York: Agathon.

Fry, G., Chantavanich, S., & Chantavanich, A. (1981). Merging quantitative and qualitative research techniques: Toward a new research paradigm. *Anthropology and Education Quarterly, 12*(2), 145–158.

Gage, N. L. (1989). The paradigm wars and their aftermath: A "historical" sketch of research on teaching since 1989. *Educational Researcher, 18,* 4–10.

Gilligan, C. (1982). *In a different voice.* Cambridge, MA: Harvard University Press.

Greenleaf, E. A. (1952). *A comparison of women at Indiana University majoring in three different colleges.* Unpublished doctoral dissertation, Indiana University, Bloomington.

Guba, E., & Lincoln, Y. S. (1981). *Naturalistic evaluation.* Beverly Hills, CA: Sage.

Heikinheimo, P. S., & Shute, J. C. M. (1986). The adaptation of foreign students: Student views and institutional implications. *Journal of College Student Personnel, 27*(5), 399–406.

Iffert, R. (1958). *Retention and withdrawal of college students.* Washington, DC: U.S. Department of Health, Education, and Welfare.

Keller, G. (1986). Free at last? Breaking the chains that bind educational research. *Review of Higher Education, 10*(2), 129–134.

Komarovsky, M. (1953). *Women in the modern world: Their education and their dilemmas.* New York: Irvington.

Kuh, G. L., Bean, J. P., Bradley, R. K., & Coomes, M. D. (1986). Contributions of student affairs journals to the literature on college students. *Journal of College Student Personnel, 27*(4), 292–304.

Leon, D. (1975). Chicano college dropouts and the educational opportunity program: Failure after high school. *High School Behavioral Science, 3,* 6–11.

Lincoln, Y. S. (1986). A future-oriented comment on the state of the profession. *Review of Higher Education, 10*(2), 135–142.

Lincoln, Y. S., & Guba, E. (1985). *Naturalistic inquiry.* Beverly Hills, CA: Sage.

Manning, K. (1989). *Campus rituals and cultural meaning.* Unpublished doctoral dissertation, Indiana University, Bloomington.

Milne, N. V. (1989). *The experiences of college students with learning disabilities.* Unpublished doctoral dissertation, Indiana University, Bloomington.

Minnesota University. (1924). Report of the Survey Commission VI: Student mortality. *Bulletin of the University of Minnesota, 4,* 27.

Olin, H. R. (1909). *The women of a state university: An illustration of the workings of coeducation in the Middle West.* New York: Putnam.

Pace, C. R. (1984). *Measuring the quality of college student experiences.* Los Angeles: University of California, Higher Education Research Institute.

Parker, C. A. (1977). On modeling reality. *Journal of College Student Personnel, 18,* 419–425.

Pascarella, E. T., Ethington, C. A., & Smart, J. C. (1988). The influence of college on humanitarian/civic involvement values. *Journal of Higher Education, 59*(4), 412–437.

Perry, W. G. (1970). *Forms of intellectual and ethical development in the college years: A scheme.* New York: Holt, Rinehart and Winston.

Powell, B., & Steelman, L. C. (1984). Variations in state SAT performance: Meaningful or misleading? *Harvard Educational Review, 54*(4), 389–412.

Rist, R. C. (1977). On the relations among educational research paradigms: From disdain to detente. *Anthropology and Education Quarterly, 8,* 42–49.

Smith, J. K. (1983). Quantitative versus qualitative research: An attempt to clarify the issue. *Educational Researcher, 12,* 6–13.

Smith, M. L. (1986). The whole is greater: Combining qualitative and quantitative approaches in evaluation studies. In D. Williams (Ed.), *Naturalistic evaluation* (New Directions for Program Evaluation, No. 30). San Francisco: Jossey-Bass.

Spradley, J. P. (1979). *The ethnographic interview.* New York: Holt, Rinehart and Winston.

Stage, F. K. (1989). College outcomes and student development: Filling the gaps. *Review of Higher Education, 12*(3), 293–304.

Stage, F. K. (1990). Research on college students: Commonality, difference, and direction. *Review of Higher Education, 13*(3), 249–258.

Stage, F. K., & Kuh, G. D. (1992). Student development in the college years. In B. Clark & G. Neave (Eds.), *Encyclopedia of higher education*. Oxford: Pergammon Press.

Strange, C. (1983). Human development theory and practice in student affairs: Ships passing in the daylight? *NASPA Journal, 21*(1), 2–8.

Terenzini, P. T. (1989). Assessment with open eyes: Pitfalls in studying student outcomes. *Journal of Higher Education, 60*(6), 644–664.

Terenzini, P. T., & Wright, T. M. (1987). Students' personal growth during the first 2 years of college. *Review of Higher Education, 10*(3), 259–271.

Tierney, W. G. (1990). *The worlds we create: Organizational aspects of Native-American participation in postsecondary education*. Unpublished manuscript, Pennsylvania State University, Center for the Study of Higher Education, University Park.

Tinto, V. (1975). Dropout from higher education: A theoretical synthesis of recent research. *Review of Educational Research, 45*, 89–125.

Whitt, E. (1989). *"Hit the ground running": Experiences of new faculty at a school of education at a research university*. Unpublished doctoral dissertation, Indiana University, Bloomington.

chapter 2

Diverse Students and Complex Issues: A Case for Multiple Methods in College Student Research

Louis C. Attinasi, Jr.
Amaury Nora

In chapter 1 Frances K. Stage presents a number of arguments for increased flexibility in our choice of methods for conducting research on and assessing college students. Underlying many of these arguments is the position that because of their extreme diversity today's college students cannot be studied adequately through the use of the structured survey instrument alone. In this chapter the authors expand this argument by examining directly the increasing diversity of the students in our institutions of higher education and its implications for research and assessment. They consider as well the complex student-related issues that researchers of college students strive to understand and the implications of this for the selection of research and assessment methods. Finally, they present some alternative research strategies for examining the experiences of diverse student bodies relative to complex issues, and illustrate their use by describing a recent series of studies that they have, independently and jointly, conducted on the persistence of Hispanic college students.

THE DIVERSITY OF THE AMERICAN COLLEGE STUDENT BODY

Background Characteristics

During the last two decades there have been dramatic changes in the face, or more accurately, faces of the American college-going population. Figures on nationwide enrollment during the period 1976–1986 compiled by the U.S. Department of Education (Editors, 1990, pp. 30–31) indicate the growing diversity of our students. According to these figures, the decade saw substantial increases in the numbers of individuals from nonmajority racial and ethnic groups and in the number of women who were enrolled in American colleges and universities. Between 1976 and 1986 the number of Native Americans enrolled in all institutions of higher education increased by 19%, the number of Hispanics by 63%, and the number of Asian Americans by 126%. After a more substantial increase in the preceding decade (1966–1976), the number of Blacks increased by 5%. In addition, the total number of women enrolled increased by 27%. (During the 10-year period the total number of men remained nearly the same, while the number of White men actually decreased by 4%.)

The increasing ethnic and racial pluralism of the American college student body can be attributed to a number of factors, particularly the civil rights activities and legislation of the 1960s and 1970s, the growth in size of the subpopulations native to the North American continent (Mexican Americans and Native Americans) and their demands for full participation in American life, and the recent waves of immigration, particularly from Southeast Asia following the Vietnam War. The greater representation of women in our student bodies certainly reflects changes in traditional views regarding educational and vocational objectives for women together with the ever-growing need of single mothers and displaced homemakers to be educated for work. The percentage of women has increased to the point that it now equals, indeed in most instances surpasses, the percentage of men in the total enrollment of institutions that enroll both men and women.

Today's college students are more diverse than their predecessors in other ways as well. For example, the numbers of students with special needs, including the physically challenged and those with learning disabilities, have grown as society's increasing sensitivity to problems of physical and educational access has been translated into legislation. In addition, older students constitute an ever-increasing percentage of higher education enrollment, reflecting both the aging of the general population and the growing trend of career changes during adulthood. Finally, the increasing availability of financial aid and targeted recruiting have resulted in the enrollment of more individuals from financially disadvantaged families.

Campus Subcultures

The students on our campuses are diverse not only in terms of the background characteristics they bring with them but also with respect to membership in student subcultures (Kuh & Whitt, 1988). Student subcultures, which are present in every institution of higher education, are based on particular "orientations" toward (Clark & Trow, 1966), or "perspectives" on (Hughes, Becker, & Geer, 1962), a college education. For example, a subculture may be oriented around a view of college as providing intellectual challenge, preparation for work, peer-group socialization, or even a place for "killing time." Campus subcultures are important because they provide their members with the means of coping with the difficulties of college life through social support and guidelines for living. They influence the way the members interpret events and problems, providing them with attitudes and values on the basis of which they "can build consistent patterns of response, enabling them to fit into the activities of the school" (Hughes et al., 1962, p. 529). Through their effects on the orientation of students toward learning and extracurricular activities, student subcultures can have profound consequences for the institutions in which they exist (Kuh & Whitt, 1988).

The variety of subcultures present on a campus are the consequence of characteristics of both the institution and its students (Kuh & Whitt, 1988). Students' precollege characteristics (e.g., values and attitudes) and prior acquaintance with one another as well as their postmatriculation characteristics (residential, class and organizational propinquity) influence the development of subcultural groups. So, too, does the institutional context, including the institutional ethos, interests of persons within the institution, authority structure, and institutional size and complexity (Clark & Trow, 1966).

Some (e.g., Clark & Trow, 1966; Katchadourian & Boli, 1985) have proposed general typologies of student subcultures. One of the best known of these is a typology developed by Clark and Trow (1966) that has four categories: the collegiate, vocational, academic, and nonconformist subcultures. A more recent typology (Katchadourian & Boli,

1985) based on a longitudinal study of Stanford University students in the early 1980s also includes four categories: the careerists, the intellectuals, the strivers, and the unconnected. Such typologies are largely heuristic or analytic devices intended to illustrate the concept of student subcultures in higher education, not descriptions of specific groups on a particular campus (Clark & Trow, 1966). Furthermore, the included categories often fail to meet generally accepted criteria for subcultures, such as persistent interaction, processes of socialization, mechanisms for social control, and norms that differ from the parent (overall institutional) culture (see Bolton & Kammayer, 1972; Horowitz, 1987; Van Maanen & Barley, 1985; Warren, 1968).

Still, typologies of student subcultures such as those proposed by Clark and Trow and Katchadourian and Boli underscore the fact that there are fundamental differences among students in their postmatriculation orientations toward a college education and begin to suggest the diversity of campus peer groups to which college students can become attached. On any particular campus, the variety of such groups is likely to be large and, at least in some respects, unique vis-à-vis what is to be found in other institutions (Clark & Trow, 1966). If, as case studies of student subcultures at particular institutions have shown (Becker, Geer, & Hughes, 1968; Becker, Geer, Hughes, & Strauss, 1961; Snyder, 1971), the influence of these subcultures is pervasive in the lives of their members, it would behoove the researcher of college students to take them fully into consideration.

RESEARCHING A DIVERSE STUDENT BODY

Students who come from different ethnic backgrounds are likely to be culturally different. Furthermore, even students who share the same ethnic culture may differ subculturally because of differences in their sex, age, physical, financial, or educational status, or their campus peer group membership. That is, we can expect that on one level (i.e., that of the general culture) the same "collective, mutually shaping patterns of norms, values, practices, beliefs, and assumptions" will be guiding their behavior and providing them with "a frame of reference within which to interpret the meaning of events and actions on and off campus" (Kuh & Whitt, 1988, pp. 12–13). On other levels (i.e., the subcultural ones), however, the shaping factors will be quite different.

Not only must the research of today's college students contend with their cultural and subcultural diversity but also with their individual subcultural, even cultural, distinctiveness. Under such circumstances the inadequacy of the structured survey instrument constructed largely from the perspective of the researcher becomes apparent. The user of such an instrument makes the assumption, albeit usually implicitly, that he or she "knows exactly what is important to ask about the college student experience," and as a consequence, the research process remains closed "to the possible emergence of hidden issues, new themes, and unpredicted discoveries" (see chapter 1). Can we expect such a data collection device alone to lead us to an understanding of the experiences of diverse students in institutions of higher education? And if not, how is the researcher of a culturally, or at least subculturally, diverse student body to proceed?

Fortunately, such a researcher has a rich research tradition upon which to draw. Cultural anthropologists have long studied groups of people culturally different from themselves with ethnography (Pelto & Pelto, 1978), a methodology appropriate for cross-cultural research. The methodology provides an insider's perspective on what is happening in the group's natural setting. (Anthropologists typically study groups in their natural settings.) This has been referred to as the *emic* perspective (Pike, 1967), and it is uncovered by research methods such as participant observation and in-depth interviewing. These methods allow the researcher to understand an experience (e.g., what it is like to be a Black student in a largely White institution) from the point of view of the experiencer himself or herself. This is accomplished without the imposition of prior researcher conceptions. It is only after uncovering the insider's perspective through "thick" qualitative data collection that the researcher then seeks to interpret his or her observations from an outsider's or *etic* perspective (Pike, 1967).

Open-ended research techniques such as participant-observation (Spradley, 1980) and in-depth interviewing (see chapter 7; Spradley, 1979) allow the researcher to study culturally different people in an open-minded (but not empty-headed) way. Initially, relative to the broad topic under investigation, anthropologists permit their informants (they prefer this term to *subjects* as it recognizes the active role of the researched in the research project) to define the relevant areas of inquiry. While recognizing that there are likely to be multiple realities—informants carry around in their heads, and act on the basis of, many different views of what is going on in the setting—they look for convergence of information. This is referred to as *triangulation* and is accomplished when different sources and/or methods of data collection inform findings. (This research strategy is discussed extensively in chapter 9.) In addition to participant-observation and in-depth interviewing, document analysis (see chapter 6) and the examination of unobtrusive informational residues (see chapter 3) are typically used in efforts to achieve triangulation.

As the study proceeds and the investigator achieves increasing triangulation of sources and methods, he or she is likely to begin focusing on some particular aspect of what is happening in the setting. This research process is often compared to a funnel: it is broad at the top, or beginning, and gradually tapers to a narrow bottom, or end. However, although some singular aspect of the setting eventually becomes the research focus, the rest is not ignored. The researcher continues to pay attention to as much of the context as he or she is able. This is because the anthropologist believes that the culture of any group is an integrated whole and that any part is incomprehensible unless interpreted relative to the whole.

An anthropologist collects and analyzes data simultaneously. Decisions about what to do next are largely based on the sense made of where he or she has already been. This refers not only to the identification of new observations to be made and new questions to be asked (and of where, when, and from whom to make or ask them) but also to the emergence and clarification of concepts and working hypotheses. The research process is largely inductive as the investigator seeks to derive more general concepts and understandings from the welter of concrete details he or she compiles. Tentative concepts and understandings are tested against the evidence resulting from a subsequent wave of data collection. Ethnographic research has often been referred to as *qualitative* since the data that are collected and analyzed are preponderantly verbal—Geertz (1973) called this "thick description"—not numerical.

It is not unusual for an anthropologist to spend 1 or 2 years in the field collecting and initially analyzing data, and then a comparable period of time in completing the analysis and writing up the results. The termination of an ethnographic study is always arbitrary, reflecting as much the exhaustion of resources—time and money—as any belief that the culture (or the particular aspect that is under investigation) is finally understood (Lincoln & Guba, 1985). The findings are typically written up as a case study (Lincoln & Guba, 1985; chapter 4) so that the ethnographer can weave a rich narrative based on what he or she has seen and heard, a narrative that captures both the emic—as much as possible the ethnographer uses the actual words of the informants themselves—and the etic perspectives on what has happened.

Wolcott (1988) drew the distinction between conducting a full-scale ethnography, on the one hand, and borrowing from the repertoire of (qualitative) methods typically employed by an ethnographer to conduct a field study that is not truly ethnographic, on the other. The distinction lies primarily in the ethnographer's attention to the broad cultural context within which the particular events of interest take place. Thus an ethnography of schooling that fails to deal with the context of schooling beyond the bounds of the school itself is not an ethnography at all.

Wolcott's distinction called attention to the fact that researchers of many stripes make use of the qualitative research techniques typically associated with ethnography. Some of these researchers come from other disciplinary backgrounds, most notably sociology, and others from no identifiable disciplinary background at all. The latter is true of many researchers who use qualitative methods to study aspects of education. The particular scholarly orientation underlying their use notwithstanding, the openness of these methods to frames of reference different from those routinely used by researchers of college students makes them particularly well suited for investigating our culturally and subculturally diverse study bodies.

THE COMPLEXITY OF STUDENT-RELATED ISSUES

Today's researcher of college students must contend not only with a diverse population of students but also with a diverse and complex set of issues. Thus, to adequately explain why college students exhibit various levels of retention and achievement, or to adequately assess their academic progress, it is necessary to consider more than one or two potentially influencing factors at a time. Reviewers of the research literature on student retention (Attinasi & Nora, 1987) have shown how the failure to do so for years slowed progress in the study of this phenomenon.

Many of the topics of interest to researchers and assessors of college students have not been examined, or are only just beginning to be examined, in terms of theoretical perspectives or conceptual frameworks. Such frameworks are often (and certainly ought to be) the basis of multifactor, explanatory models of such phenomena as college student retention and achievement. By identifying and clarifying the processes leading to various outcomes of college attendance, naturalistic research, including ethnographic inquiries, can be helpful in generating these frameworks, which then can be verified quantitatively. Moreover, such studies can generate hypotheses concerning relationships among factors in existing frameworks that can be tested through qualitative research. In addition, naturalistic research is capable of producing findings that will enhance our understanding of processes underlying cause-and-effect relationships established through quantitative research. This argues for researching student outcomes and assessing student progress with a variety of methods.

An Example: Investigations of the Retention of Hispanic Students

Student retention is one area that has been investigated by means of both naturalistic and quantitative (survey) inquiries. Duran (1987), Nora (1987), and Attinasi (1989) have all conducted studies in which the issue of the persistence of undergraduate Hispanic students, in particular, has been addressed. The use of various methodologies, (i.e., trend analysis, multivariate analysis, structural modeling, and naturalistic research) in these investigations helped to increase understanding of Hispanic student retention, an issue that is complex not only because of the complicated nature of the retention phenomenon itself but also because of the additional factor of the cultural uniqueness of Hispanics. This section now describes the various methods that have been used to investigate the retention of Hispanic students and discusses the unique contributions of qualitative (in-depth interviewing of persisters and nonpersisters) and quantitative (causal model testing with survey data) research approaches and the potential contribution of their integration.

Trend Analysis

In a study of Hispanics' precollege and undergraduate education, Duran (1987) identified specific trends related to Hispanics' participation in higher education and discussed the implications for the issues of access, retention, academic performance, and degree attainment. In particular, he documented the underrepresentation of Hispanic students relative to non-Hispanic Whites and the substantial differences between these groups in degree attainment rates, retention rates, test score level, and overall academic performance, and with respect to many other indicators of success in college. Duran did not propose potential causes of Hispanics' underrepresentation and underachievement in institutions of higher education, but his profile made clear the need to move beyond statistical description of the condition to an understanding of why the condition existed and what could be done to ameliorate it.

Many questions left unanswered by Duran's study beg to be addressed: Why are Hispanic students underrepresented in undergraduate degree attainment in all areas of higher education? Is it a matter of aspirations, high school features, institutional factors, or all of these things? Are aspirations affected by characteristics specific to 2- and 4-year institutions? What insights about the condition of Hispanic students can we obtain by talking directly and in-depth with those who are affected? Answers to these questions require both quantitative and naturalistic studies of Hispanic experiences in higher education, studies that could lead to the building and testing of theory in this area (Olivas, 1983).

A Quantitative Model

One attempt to address these questions was made by Nora (1987), who developed a quantitative causal model of student retention based on Tinto's (1975, 1987) theoretical framework and tested it with a sample of Hispanic students drawn from a 2-year college population. Nora's model includes the four key sets of variables conceptualized by Tinto to explain retention: (a) the levels of the student's integration into the academic and social lives of the institution, (b) the level of the student's commitment to an educational goal and to the institution, (c) the nature of the student's (precollege) background, and (d) a withdrawal/persistence decision. In sum, Tinto hypothesized that higher levels of social and academic integration result in higher levels of commitment both to the institution and to educational goals. The latter, in turn, increases the likelihood of persistence.

Nora used structural equation modeling to assess the appropriateness of the hypothesized causal model. The analysis provides substantiation for the relationships hypothesized in the study and indicates that the causal model is a plausible representation of influences on student retention specific to Hispanic students in 2-year institutions. Although the model can explain a good deal of the variance in Hispanic student attrition, several factors found to be significant in predicting student persistence for majority students in 4-year residential institutions do not appear to have an impact on the retention of the Hispanic community college students Nora studied.

Thus the findings are only partially supportive of the hypothesized relationship between measures of academic integration and retention found in previous retention studies. A relationship between measures of social integration and retention can not be substantiated for Hispanics in 2-year institutions, although social integration had been found to have the largest influence on withdrawal decisions for majority students. For Hispanic students, measures of initial commitments (to the institution and educational goals) have a significantly large direct effect on retention.

A Naturalistic Study

At about the same time as Nora's study, Attinasi (1989) took a different tack on the problem and conducted a naturalistic study of Hispanic retention. This was an exploratory investigation with the purpose of determining factors related to retention that could be identified through an in-depth interviewing of both persisting and nonpersisting Mexican-American students. Attinasi sought qualitative data to describe, from the student's point of view, the sociopsychological context within which he or she decided to persist or not to persist through the freshman year. In lieu of one of the existing conceptual frameworks of persistence/attrition, the inquiry was guided only by a broad research perspective, the sociology of everyday life (Douglas, 1980). This perspective focuses on everyday social interaction in natural situations and emphasizes initiating research with (a) the experience and observation of people interacting in concrete, face-to-face situations and (b) an analysis of the actors' meanings.

Data were collected through in-depth, open-ended interviewing of persisting and nonpersisting students, and analyzed inductively to generate grounded concepts for interpreting the context within which these students made persistence decisions. The analysis began with open-coding of the interview transcriptions, that is, the coding of their contents in as many ways as possible. The coding categories related to context and setting, informants' definitions of situations, informants' ways of thinking about people and objects, process (sequence of events, changes over time), activities, events, strategies, relationships, and social structure. This was followed by a data reduction step in which the number of coding categories was reduced, and the analysis began to take shape conceptually. Saliency of the categories, as judged by frequency of occurrence, uniqueness, and apparent connectedness to other categories, was the criterion for initial decisions to retain, merge, and/or discard coding categories. That is, it became possible to link categories to one another through higher order categories. A higher order category, or concept, was one under which another category could be fitted without sacrificing the latter's integrity. In this way initial coding categories became subcategories or properties of higher level categories. Eventually, connections between higher level categories were established.

From this data analysis, two conceptual schemes emerged: "getting ready" and "getting in." The getting-ready concept includes acquiring early in life through parental communication an expectation of going to college, witnessing early in life the college going of family members, having vicarious experiences of college through communications from high school teachers, and having direct experience of college through prematriculation visits to college campuses. Getting in includes postmatriculation experiences associated with the student's management of the new environment. Here two subconstructs, "getting to know" and "scaling down" emerge. Getting to know involves acquiring familiarity with the physical, social, and academic spheres of the campus through contacts with veteran students and through information sharing with fellow neophytes. Scaling down is the tendency of informants to confine their activities to narrow portions of the three campus spheres (physical, social, academic), in effect reducing the amount of new knowledge they have to acquire to successfully negotiate them. As persisters and non-persisters differ in terms of both getting-ready and getting-in experiences, Attinasi concluded that these concepts are important for understanding Hispanic student retention.

Combining Naturalistic and Quantitative Approaches

As the investigations of Hispanic student retention by Nora and Attinasi illustrate, research on college students (or the assessment of their progress) may involve either the establishment of relationships between variables (through quantitative survey methods, for example) or in-depth examination of behavioral processes (through naturalistic research methods). But it may also be desirable to integrate the two approaches in order to address the issue of unexplained variance in quantitative models and enhance understanding of relationships established between factors in these models. When tested empirically, causal models of phenomena such as college student retention and achievement typically have accounted for only a very modest amount of the variance in the behavior (e.g., persistence) of interest. The large unexplained variance associated with most of these models is probably due to either (a) the failure of the researcher to adequately operationalize the factors specified in the conceptual framework from which the model is constructed or (b) some misspecification of factors in the conceptual framework itself.

Suppose, for example, there is a conceptual framework that posits a direct effect of some factor, say commitment to the institution, on the student's persistence in the institution. Suppose further that a researcher operationalizes the conceptual framework as a quantitative causal model, measuring the commitment to the institution and persistence variables in specific ways, and then tests the causal model. If in repeated tests of the model the researcher consistently finds no direct effect of the measure(s) of commitment on the measure(s) of persistence, he or she might be tempted to conclude that a direct relationship between the factors is misspecified in the conceptual framework. This conclusion is unwarranted, however, as it is equally plausible that the failure to find a direct relationship between the factors is due to inappropriate operationalization of one or both of them in the causal model.

The exclusion of relevant variables from a causal model leads to exaggerated or underestimated effects and reduction in the variance accounted for by variables in the model (Pedhazur, 1982). Even the exclusion of variables that are not correlated with other variables in the model can have adverse effects because, by increasing error terms (unexplained variance), such exclusion can distort the relationships between the included variables (Pedhazur, 1982).

One way to reduce the size of the error terms associated with existing quantitative models of college student outcomes such as persistence is to begin to incorporate into these models findings from naturalistic research (Fry, Chantavanich, & Chantavanich, 1981). Naturalistic research has the potential for identifying factors that influence outcomes that will otherwise remain unidentified, hence unmeasured, and thus subsumed under error terms. The inclusion of these omitted factors in conceptual models, and of appropriate measures of them in causal models, should not only reduce the risk of specification error but also increase our understanding of the processes underlying relationships established in these models.

The above logic led Nora, Attinasi, and Matonak (1990) to undertake a study seeking to improve the explanatory capacity of a quantitative model. The study combined Tinto's (1975, 1987) framework for explaining retention with some of the qualitative factors Attinasi (1989) identified in his naturalistic investigation. The result was a causal model that includes new measures of Tinto's background component based on Attinasi's getting-ready concept. It was tested through path analysis on a sample of academically underprepared students drawn from a community college population.

Most previous studies found, contrary to Tinto's conceptualization, that the precollege background of students has little or no direct effect on persistence decisions. The previous failure to find such an effect could be due to the failure to operationalize the background factor appropriately. Measures based on the getting-ready concept might specify the precollege component better and allow us to confirm a direct effect of it on retention.

The new causal model has a good overall fit to the data in explaining the variance in both integration and retention factors. The getting-ready measures affect positively and directly the two major intervening variables in the model: social integration and academic integration. However, contrary to what was hypothesized, they have a significant negative direct effect on retention itself, perhaps because the getting-ready measures are based on university students oriented principally to the 4-year institution. We may expect that the greater the number and intensity of these experiences the more quickly the decision will be made to transfer out of the community college.

In any event, this study illustrates the potential of combining naturalistic and quantitative methods to investigate college student outcomes. The findings of Attinasi's interview study suggest a new, perhaps better, operationalization of the background component of Tinto's theoretical framework. It is not difficult to conceive of improved measurement of other factors in Tinto's framework (and factors in other models of retention and other phenomena) through the findings of naturalistic research, which would be subsequently tested with survey data. Naturalistic research also has the potential for providing in-depth understanding of relationships between factors that are well established through the testing of causal models with survey data. For example, although we might have established a statistically significant relationship between particular quantitative measures of, say, social integration and persistence through causal model testing, we might still wish to understand how the relationship plays itself out in the everyday life of individual students; after all, there is only so much of human behavior that can ultimately be captured in numbers. To achieve such understanding is the object of naturalistic research.

CONCLUSION

In this chapter we have described both the increasing diversity of American college students and the complexity of the issues typically addressed by those who conduct research on them. Both have implications for research methods. The cultural and subcultural diversity of students calls for the use of methods that allow the researcher to be sensitive to diverse frames of reference, many of which may be quite different from the investigator's own. A standardized questionnaire developed from the researcher's own frame of reference will not adequately capture the experiences and attitudes of students who have diverse racial or ethnic backgrounds or who are subculturally diverse due to differences in age, sex, special needs, financial status, or campus peer group affiliation. Rather, the researcher also needs to be able to draw upon the rich research methodology developed by anthropologists and others who have traditionally engaged in cross-cultural research. The researcher needs to ground his or her understanding of what happens to students in college in the students' own understanding of these events.

The complexity of potential issues—for example, retention and achievement—also argues for the use of a variety of methods, both naturalistic and quantitative, in the research and assessment of college students. To understand student retention or achievement requires both the development and testing of multifactor quantitative models and detailed understanding of student perceptions of influences on these outcomes. The findings of naturalistic approaches can both assist in the development of the conceptual frameworks from which quantitative models are drawn and illuminate our understanding of the processes that underlie associations identified in these models. The authors have used their own independent and joint investigations of the retention of undergraduate Hispanic students to illustrate the potential of this kind of multiple-method approach for studying a unique cultural group.

FURTHER READING

For further reading on the experiences of diverse college students, see particularly Fleming's *Blacks in College* (1984), Olivas' *Latino College Students* (1986), or *Evolving Theoretical Perspectives on College Students* (1990), edited by Moore. (For complete publications data, see the reference list.)

REFERENCES

Attinasi, L. C., Jr. (1989). Getting in: Mexican Americans' perceptions of university attendance and the implications for freshman year persistence. *Journal of Higher Education, 60,* 247–277.

Attinasi, L. C., Jr., & Nora, A. (1987, November). *The next step in the study of student persistence in college.* Paper presented at the meeting of the Association for the Study of Higher Education, Baltimore, MD.

Becker, H. S., Geer, B., & Hughes, E. C. (1968). *Making the grade: The academic side of college life.* New York: Wiley.

Becker, H. S., Geer, B., Hughes, E C., & Strauss, A. L. (1961). *Boys in white.* Chicago: University of Chicago Press.

Bolton, C. D., & Kammayer, K. C. W. (1972). Campus cultures, role orientations, and social types. In K. Feldman (Ed.), *College and student: Selected readings in the social psychology of higher education.* New York: Pergamon.

Clark, B. R., & Trow, M. (1966). The organizational context. In T. M. Newcomb & E. K. Wilson (Eds.), *College peer groups: Problems and prospects for research.* Chicago: Aldine.

Douglas, J. D. (1980). Introduction to the sociologies of everyday life. In J. D. Douglas, *Introduction to the sociologies of everyday life* (pp. 1–19). Boston: Allyn & Bacon.

Duran, R. P. (1987). Hispanics' precollege and undergraduate education: Implications for science and engineering students. In L. S. Dix (Ed.), *Minorities: Their underrepresentation and career differentials in science and engineering* (pp. 73–128). Washington, DC: National Academy.

Editors of *The Chronicle of Higher Education.* (1990). *The almanac of higher education 1989–1990.* Chicago: University of Chicago Press.

Fleming, J. (1984). *Blacks in college: A comparative study of students' success in Black and White institutions.* San Francisco: Jossey-Bass.

Fry, G., Chantavanich, S., & Chantavanich, A. (1981). Merging quantitative and qualitative research techniques: Toward a new research paradigm. *Anthropology and Education Quarterly, 12,* 145–148.

Geertz, C. (1973). *The interpretation of cultures.* New York: Basic Books.

Horowitz, H. L. (1987). *Campus life: Undergraduate cultures from the end of the 18th century to the present.* New York: Knopf.

Hughes, E. C., Becker, H. S., & Geer, B. (1962). Student culture and academic effort. In N. Sanford (Ed.), *The American college.* New York: Wiley.

Katchadourian, H. A., & Boli, J. (1985). *Careerism and intellectualism among college students.* San Francisco: Jossey-Bass.

Kuh, G. D., & Whitt, E. J. (1988). *The invisible tapestry: Culture in American colleges and universities* (ASHE-ERIC Higher Education Report No. 1). Washington, DC: Association for the Study of Higher Education.

Lincoln, Y., & Guba, E. (1985). *Naturalistic inquiry.* Beverly Hills, CA: Sage.

Moore, L. (1990). *Evolving theoretical perspectives on students* (New Directions for Student Services, No. 51). San Francisco: Jossey-Bass.

Nora, A. (1987). Determinants of retention among Chicano college students: A structural model. *Research in Higher Education, 26,* 31–59.

Nora, A., Attinasi, L. C., Jr., & Matonak, A. (1990). Testing qualitative indicators of precollege factors in Tinto's attrition model: A community college population. *Review of Higher Education, 13,* 337–356.

Olivas, M. A. (1983). Research and theory on Hispanic education: Students, finance, and governance. *Atzalan, 14,* 111–146.

Olivas, M. (1986). *Latino college students.* New York: Teacher's College Press.

Pedhazur, E. J. (1982). *Multiple regression in behavioral research* (2nd ed.). New York: Holt, Rinehart and Winston.

Pelto, P. J., & Pelto, G. H. (1978). *Anthropological research: The structure of inquiry* (2nd ed.). New York: Cambridge University Press.

Pike, K. L. (1967). *Language in relation to a unified theory of the structure of human behavior.* Hague: Mouton.

Snyder, B. R. (1971). *The hidden curriculum.* Cambridge: M.I.T. Press.

Spradley, J. P. (1979). *The ethnographic interview.* New York: Holt, Rinehart and Winston.

Spradley, J. P. (1980). *Participant observation.* New York: Holt, Rinehart and Winston.

Tinto, V. (1975). Dropout from higher education: A theoretical synthesis of recent research. *Review of Educational Research, 45,* 89–125.

Tinto, V. (1987). *Student leaving: Rethinking the causes and cures of student attrition.* Chicago: University of Chicago Press.

Van Maanen, J., & Barley, S. R. (1985). Occupational communities: Culture and control in organizations. *Research in Organizational Behavior, 6,* 287–365.

Warren, J. R. (1968). Student perceptions of college subcultures. *American Educational Research Journal, 5,* 213–232.

Wolcott, H. F. (1988). Ethnographic research in education. In R. M. Jaeger (Ed.), *Complementary methods for research in education* (pp. 187–206). Washington, DC: American Educational Research Association.

chapter 3

Validating Results With Nonreactive Measures

Ruth V. Russell

College students are researched and assessed frequently and extensively. Whether the inquiry motivation is a pilot exploration of new methods using college students as a convenience sample, or understanding college students as a unique group, researchers from numerous disciplines have at least some data on college students. Inquiry about college and university students from the psychologist, the sociologist, the economist, the educator, the political scientist, and others converges to provide a rich profile of this population's characteristics, preferences, motives, behaviors, and attitudes that researchers and administrators in student affairs and higher education can utilize.

What are the factors that predict a student's choice of college major? What types of promotional literature are most persuasive to potential college attenders? What facilities and programs enhance the quality of campus life for students? What role do faculty play in student attrition? What services enable historically underrepresented groups of students to succeed in college? Answers to these questions may be found in great abundance in the research literature of a diverse array of social and psychological science subject areas. Questionnaires, personal interviews, psychometric tests, experiments, and other customary methods are the typical sources of information on college students. Yet, most often these measurement techniques, and the motives behind them, are obvious to students and others responding to them, for example, professors and administrators. In addition, within a particular discipline, there often will be a habitual preference for one type of measure, such as a psychometric test in psychology or questionnaire in education, ignoring alternatively useful measures.

Webb and his colleagues (Webb, Campbell, Schwartz, & Sechrest, 1966; Webb, Campbell, Schwartz, Sechrest, & Grove, 1981) wrote extensively on the hazards of overreliance on a single measurement strategy. They particularly lamented the overdependence by social scientists and others on interviews and questionnaires. Others have agreed by warning about the inherent limitations of overdependence on a particular data collection method. For example, in writing about research from the student affairs literature, Abler and Sedlacek (1988) described interviews and questionnaires as time consuming and expensive. The time and money needed for constructing and scoring questionnaires and conducting interviews, or the printing costs and supplies, often are prohibitive, especially at the beginning of a research effort.

A far more important problem is, however, that interviews, questionnaires, and other standard measurement strategies intrude as a foreign element into the situation they describe. They set into motion new attitudes and elicit atypical responses from subjects. Such methods were labeled *reactive* by Webb and associates because the subject's reaction to the methodology influences his or her responses. This can invalidate research or assessment results; when people know their actions or words are being counted, they do not always respond accurately or normally. Thus interviews, questionnaires, tests, and experiments can create as well as measure responses. For example, a questionnaire that asks college students about their attitudes toward students from other cultures can inspire, at least temporarily, more positive attitudes than usual simply because the responding students are aware of the "desirable" response.

Abler and Sedlacek (1988) discussed the danger of the reactivity of measurement with another example. Suppose athletic administrators want to examine the degree of racial discrimination present in a college sports program. Further suppose that to answer their questions, they interview coaches and athletes about the alleged problem and administer various racial attitude questionnaires.

> Given the demand characteristics of the situation (coaches—the desire for their programs to appear in a positive light; athletes—pressure not to jeopardize their athletic careers), however, the racial problems are minimized, and, receiving these results, the administration continues current policies when more accurate information would have suggested changes be made. (pp. 158–159)

To validate such obtrusive measures, Webb et al. (1981) proposed adding unobtrusive, or nonreactive, ways of gathering data to the research design. Whereas reactive measures either call upon the research subjects to respond to a stimulus presented by the researcher (for instance, a question or a task), or to cooperate with the researcher by carrying on "as usual" while their "natural" behavior is being observed, nonreactive measures call upon the researcher either to find naturally occurring data, to observe unobtrusively, or to create situations in which the subjects are unaware of being parties to research (Brewer & Hunter, 1989). A researcher employing nonreactive methods seeks to avoid influencing the subjects in even the slightest way, including altering environmental conditions (Kraus & Allen, 1987).

This is not a difficult approach; most people are unaware that they collect information nonreactively every day. The number of transcripts sent to other undergraduate institutions by the registrar's office may help assess student satisfaction. The case loads in the student health center and psychological counseling service help indicate the amount and timing of stress on campus. Library usage rates reveal something about students' intellectual curiosity.

The point is that these nonreactive measures can offer an additional source of information about college student outcomes that serves a legitimate and important measurement role. Despite this, nonreactive methods are not used systematically in most research on college students, and their importance has been understated.

This chapter provides an overview of nonreactive measures and illustrates their incorporation into research and assessment on college students. The purpose is to stimulate readers to think more carefully about nonreactive measures and to begin to plan for their use when appropriate.

RATIONALE FOR NONREACTIVE MEASURES

Used simultaneously with more typical measures of studying college students, nonreactive measures can provide a validation of measurement on the phenomenon of interest. No data collection approach is without bias. There is more than one way of knowing. Adding nonreactive measures to a research design increases confidence in those data that may be similar even though they emanate from different measurement methods. Thus nonreactive measures are proposed as a supplement to more traditional measurement methods because of differences in validity. Measurement of student beliefs about altruism, for example, is more likely to be well grounded or cogent if assessed not only by questionnaires and interviews that ask about this belief but also by nonreactively counting memberships in civic and humanitarian student organizations.

Every assessment or research technique carries with it certain sources of error. This error exists in different ways and to different degrees. On one hand, the errors are constant within types of measures; the direction and size of the error are assumed to be fixed for a given set of measurement strategies (Sechrest & Phillips, 1979). On the other hand, the direction of errors is also random across procedures. "For any given measurement task, the errors are additive: an error in one direction will tend to cancel out an error in the other direction" (Sechrest & Phillips, 1979, p. 2).

Much of the reason for using nonreactive measures involves the ability to avoid the same sources of invalidity or errors inherent in other types of measures. Even though nonreactive measures have their own innate biases, they counterbalance the systematic error characteristics of standard procedures, such as interviews and questionnaires, because their bias is different. Goodwin and Goodwin (1989) summarized two categories of sources of measurement invalidity in reactive measures that nonreactive measures avoid: error due to the respondent and error due to the investigator.

- *Invalidity due to the respondent.* Invalidity situations that are due to the respondent, a source of error for many types of measures but minimized by nonreactive measures, include:

  1. *Awareness of being tested.* Subjects being assessed may reply or act in an unusual fashion because there is focus on them. Such a "guinea pig effect" can result in abnormal behaviors or responses. College students who are studied frequently may become bored and thus be lazy in giving responses, or those who are newcomers to serving as research respondents may be self-conscious and give incomplete or inaccurate responses.

  2. *Role selection.* Persons being measured, researched, or evaluated must decide what role they should play during the process. Orne (1962) demonstrated that subjects place themselves into false roles as they try to be "good subjects" and please the experimenter or "bad subjects" and turn the research effort into a game. Special instructions on questionnaires or tests such as "it is important that you do your best" or "you are part of a special group selected to do this" actually may elevate the measure's reactivity. For example, if the researcher asks students how well they like the food in the residence hall, some may give exaggeratedly negative responses. Or international students may respond to

questions from college authorities in positive ways fearing that their actual, more negative response may result in repercussions. Nonreactive measures can counterbalance such sources of invalidity.

3. *Measurement itself as a change agent.* This threat to validity occurs when the data collection method produces real changes in what is being measured. A well-known example is pretest sensitization (Campbell & Stanley, 1963), in which the questions alter the subject's attitude or sensitize the subject to attend to certain specific elements of the treatment to follow. For example, college students might score higher on a racial awareness scale if they have previously taken the scale, even without the treatment; they have "learned" from the first testing.

4. *Response sets.* A final measurement error due to the respondent, which could be minimized by nonreactive measures, involves tendencies to respond in a particular way regardless of the question asked. One type of response set, acquiescence, involves agreeing more often with a positive statement than disagreeing with the same statement when it is phrased negatively. Other response sets include preferences for strongly worded statements over moderate or indecisive ones and tendencies to endorse a particular response pattern (such as all third responses). Many college students have learned how teachers devise tests and have developed useful strategies for answering in a desirable, automatic fashion.

- *Invalidity due to the researchers.* Sources of potential invalidity or error in traditional measurement tools due to the researcher, as outlined by Goodwin and Goodwin (1989), include:

  1. *Characteristics of the researcher.* Threats to the validity of a measure can include such researcher qualities as age, race, sex, physical size, apparent social class, culture, and occupation. Imagine, for example, how a college student might react to an interviewer who is a college administrator as opposed to one who is a fellow college student. Additional elements involved in this source of error are the researcher's tone of voice, the precise wording of each question if asked orally, and even the order in which questions are asked.

  2. *Change in the measurement instrument.* A second possible source of invalidity that nonreactive measures avoid may occur when the measuring instrument is an interviewer. Over time, an interviewer can become more skilled, more in command of the needed vocabulary, more able to establish rapport, or more bored.

Although nonreactive measures are not free of their own sources of invalidity, they increase confidence in the validity of the study when they yield similar results as reactive methods. Such convergence of findings about a particular phenomenon among alternative assessment methods elevates a study's believability.

TYPES OF NONREACTIVE MEASURES

What is it about nonreactive measures that enables them to counter the potential invalidity just presented? Webb et al. (1981) characterized nonreactive methods according to the three basic types: physical traces, archives, and observation.

Physical Traces

Physical tracing concerns visible evidence of preceding behavior. These are pieces of data, or traces, not specifically produced for research but nonetheless available to be exploited opportunistically by the investigator. The debris from a fraternity party provides a trace about what went on; graffiti in campus restrooms offer a clue to student political attitudes; food wastage in the cafeteria adds to our knowledge of menu popularity; worn strips of grass indicate preferred student walking patterns across campus. Physical traces are inconspicuous and anonymous in that the generator of them has no knowledge of their potential research use (Goodwin & Goodwin, 1989).

Webb et al. (1981) discriminate between two broad classes of physical traces. On the one hand, there are *erosion physical traces*, where the degree of selective wear on some material yields the measure. Such a measure could be the wear over time displayed on floor tile in front of various student union exhibits or bulletin boards as an index to each exhibit's popularity. The degree of concern by students about AIDS could be measured by the rate at which informational brochures about the disease need to be replenished in the display area at the student health center.

On the other hand, there are *accretion physical traces*. These traces involve the deposit or accumulation of material. For example, counting the number of alcohol containers left in the football stadium after the game could indicate students' level of compliance with the administration's "no containers" policy. The contents of informal bulletin boards throughout campus might add to data about the intellectual or political tenor of a student body.

Although including physical trace measures in a research design might enthuse the Sherlock Holmes in all of us, there are limitations to their usefulness. First, certain accretion measures vary substantially in their survivability and in their tendency to be deposited. Archeologists have noted that materials vary in durability (e.g., graffiti vs. paper trash), and more valuable materials are less likely to be deposited. Also, many variables influence the nature of traces left. For instance, graffiti appearing in some places may be more delicate than those in other places out of a desire to be inoffensive, which outweighs any desire to express deeper sentiments (Sechrest & Phillips, 1979). Another limitation is the extensive time typically required to collect some forms of trace measures, such as the wear on new floor tiles. A final limitation is the scant knowledge available about the persons producing the traces; their anonymity, the very nonreactivity of the measure, prohibits us from knowing anything else about them. What did the students observe most as they stood in front of the display case? Were men or women more drawn to the display? What were their reactions? Did the display change an attitude or behavior?

Archives

The second type of nonreactive measure suggested by Webb et al. (1981) is archival—documents and records. Two forms of archival data are the ongoing (running, continuing, or routine) documents and episodic (private) records. Continuous records tend to be public; examples include actuarial records (e.g., birth, death, marriage), political and judicial records (e.g., votes, court proceedings), other government records (e.g., city budgets), crime records, mass media archives, and some institutional data (e.g., admissions figures). Private records tend to be more discontinuous and seldom are in the public domain. Examples include personal documents (e.g., diaries, letters, drawings), sales records, and certain kinds of institutional records (e.g., attendance, grade, and disciplinary action files).

One archival indicator of student patterns of social conservatism could be a charting across years of the topics about which students choose to write in an introductory sociology class. Other illustrations appropriate to college student inquiry include an assessment of the book titles most frequently checked out at the library as a rough clue of literary sophistication; parental attendance during orientation sessions for new students as a measure of the extent of parental interest and support; and the number, size, and participation rates in formal student organizations that have some specific academic purpose, as compared with clubs that have athletic, entertainment, or social purposes, as indicator of the importance students attach to the life of the mind. Similarly, inferences about the relative emphasis given to the academic and social life of a campus might be made based on an examination of the content of campus concert, film, lecture, and speaker series.

As suggested by Terenzini (1986), the distribution of courses taken by size and type of instruction (e.g., lecture, seminar, lab, independent study) might reveal the nature of the formal educational process experienced by students. For example, how many opportunities were there for graduating seniors to study in small numbers with a faculty member? As another example, Blackburn, Armstrong, Conrad, Didham, and McKune (1976) undertook a national study of changes in degree requirements between 1967 and 1974. They explored the amount, structure, and content of general education as well as the structure and flexibility in selected major degree requirements. They found the typical baccalaureate degree recipient in 1974 had taken about 22% less coursework in general education than did his or her 1967 counterpart.

Green, Prather, and Sturgeon (1983) used nonreactive measurement to evaluate the performance of college teachers. The indicator was the degree to which teachers developed a following among students, measured by how often students returned to teachers for additional courses.

Most colleges and universities are wealthy with archival data, and when used in conjunction with other methods, these administrative data can add to a study's validity. Limitations of archival records, however, are authenticity, representativeness, and accuracy (Goodwin & Goodwin, 1989).

Authenticity concerns whether the records are real. What is the history of the document? How was it obtained? Was it complete or abridged? Representativeness concerns the record's ability to yield a true likeness of the issue. Such factors as selective recording and selective survival affect the representativeness of the record. For example, letters praising a college or an academic unit are more faithfully filed than are critical letters. Also, how certain statistics are kept by organizations can change across time. Finally, the accuracy of archival records is of particular importance. Who prepared the records, using what information sources, and for what purpose? The biases of the author or the perspective of the organization preparing the record could be crucial.

Observation

A third type of nonreactive measure, observation, simply refers to watching behavior without the knowledge of the subjects. To be unobtrusive, a student being observed must be unaware of the measurement purpose. Two approaches to unobtrusive observation suggested by Webb et al. (1981) are *simple observation* and *contrived observation*.

Simple observation requires that the observer has no control over the behavior being observed and plays a passive role in the situation. Exterior physical signs such as type, length, fabric, and size of students' clothing, or expressive movements such as body language and facial expressions, could be observed. Simple observation also may include noting seating patterns in class, alcohol-induced behaviors at sporting events, and physical proximity of students on grassy commons areas on campus. Timing how long certain behaviors persist, counting name-calling incidents, and the like all provide opportunities for passive observation.

For example, if an institution wished to know the extent to which racial openness was a characteristic trait of the student body, a researcher might design a study similar to that reported by Campbell, Kruskal, and Wallace (1966). In that study, the tendency of White and Black students to sit by themselves in racially homogeneous groups in classrooms was studied. Variations on this approach might include a study of clusters of students in dining halls and cafeterias, or in library study spaces, according to race or gender or nationality (as demonstrated by Heikinheimo & Shute, 1986).

Limitations of simple observation include the chance that much of what is observed may not be relevant. Further, only limited random sampling normally is possible, and populations available for observation fluctuate by time and location (Goodwin & Goodwin, 1989). Too, many settings are private and simply unavailable for observation.

Contrived observation involves an active measurer who deliberately varies the setting or uses mechanical devices rather than human observers. Still, these interventions are nonreactive: subjects do not detect them and the apparent naturalness of the situation is preserved. As illustration, Tyson, Schlachter, and Cooper (1988) examined the racial discrimination of South African students using a game playing strategy. Observing the behaviors of racially mixed game teams, Tyson et al. concluded that both Black and White students cooperated to a greater extent with a Black co-player, revealing to the researchers a paternalistic approach on the part of some White players and apparent reverse discrimination.

Mechanical recording devices improve on simple observation as they circumvent the frailties of the human observer and create a permanent record that permits coder reliability checks. A variety of measuring devices, such as one-way mirrors, still and movie cameras, television cameras and recorders, tape recorders, infrared film, radio transmitters, bugging devices, and eye or body movement recording devices are available.

Contrived observation also has limitations. Despite advances in making recording equipment smaller and more mobile, some equipment remains large and obvious. Further, equipment costs and especially the costs of analyzing tapes and films can quickly become prohibitive. Reporting results can be difficult and expensive too, if actual photographs, films, or tapes are involved. The most important limitation, however, concerns a host of ethical issues that often accompany the use of contrived observations. These issues are discussed at the end of the chapter.

A DEMONSTRATION IN STUDENT AFFAIRS

The three types of nonreactive measures (physical traces, archives, and observation) provide distinct advantages to the researcher, but each has limitations. The primary rationale for such measures remains; their use as supplementary measures ameliorates an overreliance on any single, or primary, method. As one component of a multimethod design, nonreactive methods are especially useful because of their relative freedom from the same sources of error that threaten reactive methods. In this section, a prototype of a student affairs/higher education study demonstrates this rationale and the operationalization of nonreactive measures.

Suppose we are interested in studying the alienation of international students from the life of our campus. Because there are large numbers of international students in U.S. colleges and universities, there is growing concern about the effect of alienation on retention, academic success, and satisfaction with time spent in the United States.

In checking the literature we learn that several variables have been discussed as related to alienation among international students. We hypothesize that less alienated students are likely to be those who are male, live with a spouse, are older, come from Europe and an urban location, are studying at a graduate level, have been in the United States for a relatively longer period of time, and have extensive social contact with Americans (Schram & Lauver, 1988).

To investigate the level of alienation on our campus, we decide upon the following procedure. We randomly select the names of 200 international students from our registrar's list. We mail to them two questionnaires: one that elicits demographic information and another that measures feelings of alienation and levels of social contact. In the demographic questionnaire we ask about marital status, home country, home town size, gender, and length of stay in the United States. On the alienation and social contact questionnaire the international students are asked questions about those with whom they generally spend their time outside class and how frequently, social interactions with faculty, and involvement in campus activities as well as items assessing powerlessness, meaninglessness, and social estrangement.

Suppose, however, we are worried that the respondents might overstate their frequency of social contacts in order to make their academic work and progress in America seem successful. Or perhaps we suspect they may understate their feelings of estrangement to avoid appearing a social failure in the eyes of others, particularly those at home.

To help counteract these problems, we supplement the questionnaires with nonreactive methods. Possible options include (1) unobtrusively observing the group make-up (race and group size) of students during randomly chosen time periods in the campus cafeteria, (2) studying the client records from the student counseling center to determine frequency and nature of usage by international students as compared to other students, (3) counting the number of international students in noninternational-focused campus clubs, and (4) assessing the proportion of international students in campus social clubs with members from primarily their own home culture.

In reporting our results and drawing conclusions, the data derived from the nonreactive methodology are treated the same as those from the questionnaires. Suppose, for example, we find from our questionnaires that students from Asia, followed by those from Africa, have higher alienation scores than students from the Middle East. And students from West European countries have the lowest alienation scores. We express this result, most likely, by reporting the means and standard deviations, and calculating correlational statistics between these scores and other demographic information.

Also imagine that from studying the student counseling center records we learn that African and Middle Eastern students are more likely to receive psychological counseling. From studying the composition of noninternational-student-focused campus social clubs we learn that Asian students are least represented. In handling these data, we can again use descriptive statistics such as means, standard deviations, percentages, proportions, and others. For example, we could report the percentages of students utilizing psychological counseling services according to nationality, or the mean number of international students involved in noninternational-focused clubs.

The conclusions for our report likewise should reflect the total data set. That is, Asian students are most likely to experience alienation on our campus and less likely to go to campus-sponsored units for support or help. In addition to discussing the potential inaccuracies in our questionnaire data due to potential over- or underresponses, we must also report the potential inaccuracies in our nonreactive method derived data. For example, it may not be easy for the unobtrusive observer to properly identify the race or ethnicity of student groupings in the cafeteria.

CAVEATS

Nonreactive measurement enables the unobtrusive collection of naturally occurring data about college students. In comparison to more overt and direct measuring procedures, nonreactive techniques entail less risk that subjects will react abnormally to measurement and do not require subjects' knowing cooperation with the research in order to generate data. These methods reduce the risk of errors stemming from the bias effects of studying only cooperative subjects in unnatural situations (Brewer & Hunter, 1989).

Yet, as has been mentioned, nonreactive methods are not without their own dangers, and as a final comment, a warning is issued. The major risks of including any nonreactive measurement in a research design are validity and ethics.

First, an important concern for using nonreactive methods is that the data collected nonreactively might not actually measure the variable of focus. Does the occupancy rate in residence halls on weekends really indicate the role of the college in students' lives? Because the researcher remains unobtrusive, respondents cannot be asked about the meaning of the data they provide (Abler & Sedlacek, 1988).

For example, in studying racial discrimination in a college athletic program (McGehee & Paul, 1984), a simple nonreactive approach might be to use team records to review the racial make-up of the teams. Do any patterns emerge with respect to what positions are played by minorities? Have minority players ever consistently assumed leadership roles such as quarterback? In concluding that discrimination does exist, there is a risk that the data do not mean this at all. Alternate explanations for the racial make-ups of past teams might be that the school has difficulty attracting minority athletes or that no minority quarterbacks were available to be recruited.

Although the strength of nonreactive measurement lies in its ability to obtain naturally occurring data unobtrusively, a weakness is the limited access to explanatory information or the control of other variables because of this nonreactivity. Nonreactive data can thus require more extrapolation and interpretation on the part of the researcher. Data on college students collected in this manner are rarely complete and often inaccurate owing to natural social biases (for instance, the variability with which colleges keep records).

> On the one hand, nonreactive methods can result in misleading data
> if researchers make tenuous extrapolations from the data to the con-
> struct of interest and do not explore alternate explanations; question-
> naires and interviews are not as prone to this problem because they can
> request the information of interest more directly. Alternatively, ques-
> tionnaires and interviews potentially result in inaccurate information
> because of participant reaction to the data collection procedures; non-
> reactive measure provide data free of the confound. (Abler & Sedlacek,
> 1988, p. 161)

The solution, of course, is in the use of nonreactive methods not as a replacement of other research methods but rather to supplement and cross-validate them.

Ethical considerations are also of prime concern in the use of non-reactive methods. Are privacy and the right to informed consent violated when subjects are not aware of the data collection? Generally speaking, researchers are properly reluctant to make surreptitious observations, just as they are reluctant to perform experiments involving deception (West & Gunn, 1978). However, just as with deception experiments, there are difficult issues of data quality raised by the necessity of inform-ing respondents that they are to be observed.

Webb et al. (1981) offered some guidelines for overcoming these ethical questions. They concluded that the right to privacy falls on a continuum, from observing public behavior of public figures to spying on private behavior in private places. It was clear to them that one continuum extreme is not an invasion of privacy and the other extreme is. The area in the middle of the continuum, however, provokes the most controversy. A key question for Webb and his associates was whether the people being observed clearly expect that their behavior will be unregarded. For example, observations in public campus restrooms might be considered an invasion of privacy because students and faculty enter such restrooms with the expectation "that their be-havior will be studiously ignored" even though they are labeled *public* (Webb et al., 1981, p. 147).

The position of Sechrest and Phillips (1979) was that public behavior should be observable by any means that protect what might be termed *assumed privacy*, the privacy that one might expect from being at a distance from others or of being screened from usual views. Thus special listening devices, powerful binoculars, or peepholes would be regarded as invasions of privacy. However, whether students have a right to walk across campus without having observers note their physical proximity or their touching of each other remains a gray area. As Sechrest and Phillips (1979) suggested, "in the course of what is clearly a developing ethic of social scientific study, unobtrusive measures will have to come

in for their share of scrutiny along with all other methods of inquiry"
(p. 15).

Informed consent also poses a difficult ethical question for researchers using nonreactive methods because informed consent from students
that occurs before the study can result in reactive responses. In certain
cases, it also may be difficult to determine from whom to obtain consent
and what is an acceptable agreement to participate in the study. Whether
or not any entrapment can occur as well as the degree of risk involved
for any participant are also important considerations (Abler & Sedlacek,
1988). Webb et al. (1981) therefore supported the use of review boards
and other scientific community expert panels as a means of providing
guidance.

CONCLUSION

The case for nonreactive measures in college student assessment and
research is strong. As stated by Brown (1986), it is important for student
affairs and higher education professionals to continue to expand their
research efforts. Nonreactive measures can have a useful confirmatory
role in this expansion. So after you have scored the questionnaires, get
out of that office and on to the campus and see what is really going on!

FURTHER READING

A primary source for additional information and instruction on nonreactive measures is the second edition of *Nonreactive Measures in the Social
Sciences* by E. K. Webb, D. T. Campbell, L. Schwart, L. Sechrest, and J.
B. Grove, published by Houghton Mifflin in 1981. The chapter "Unobtrusive measures: An overview" by L. Sechrest and M. Phillips is also a
useful basic resource. It was published in 1979 in *Unobtrusive Measurement
Today: New Directions for Methodology of Behavior Science*, with L. Sechrest
as editor, by Jossey-Bass.

REFERENCES

Abler, R. M., & Sedlacek, W. E. (1988). Nonreactive measures in student affairs
   research. *Journal of College Student Development, 29*, 158–162.
Blackburn, R., Armstrong, E., Conrad, C., Didham, J., & McKune, I. (1976).
   Changing practices in undergraduate education. Berkeley, CA: Carnegie Council
   on Policy Studies in Higher Education.

Brewer, J., & Hunter, A. (1989). *Multimethod research: A synthesis of styles.* Newbury Park, CA: Sage.

Brown, R. (1986). Research: A frill or an obligation? *Journal of College Student Personnel, 27,* 195.

Campbell, D. T., & Stanley, J. S. (1963). *Experimental and quasi-experimental designs for research.* Skokie, IL: Rand McNally.

Campbell, D. T., Kruskal, W. H., & Wallace, W. P. (1966). Seating aggregation as an index of attitude. *Sociometry, 29,* 1–15.

Goodwin, W. L., & Goodwin, L. D. (1989). The use of nonreactive measures with preschoolers. *Early Child Development and Care, 41,* 173–194.

Green, J. E., Prather, J. E., & Sturgeon, J. (1983). *Using administrative data as unobtrusive indicators of teaching performance.* Paper presented at the Annual Forum of the Association for Institutional Research, Toronto, Ontario.

Heikinheimo, P. S., & Shute, J. C. M. (1986). The adaptation of foreign students: Student views and institutional implications. *Journal of College Student Personnel, 27,* 399–406.

Kraus, R., & Allen, L. (1987). *Research and evaluation in recreation, parks, and leisure studies.* Columbus, OH: Publishing Horizons.

McGehee, R., & Paul, M. (1984). *Racial make-up of central stacking and other playing positions in Southeastern Conference football teams, 1967–1983.* Paper presented at the Conference on Sport and Society, Clemson University, Clemson, SC.

Orne, M. T. (1962). On the social psychology of the experiment: With particular reference to demand characteristics and their implications. *American Psychologist, 17,* 776–783.

Schram, J. L., & Lauver, P. J. (1988). Alienation in international students. *Journal of College Student Development, 29,* 146–150.

Sechrest, L., & Phillips, M. (1979). Unobtrusive measures: An overview. In L. Sechrest (Ed.) *Unobtrusive measurement today: New directions for methodology of behavior science.* San Francisco: Jossey-Bass.

Terenzini, P. T. (1986). *The case for unobtrusive measures.* Paper presented at the ETS Invitational Conference, New York City.

Tyson, G. A., Schlachter, A., & Cooper, S. (1988). Game playing strategy as an indicator of racial prejudice among South African students. *Journal of Social Psychology, 128,* 473–485.

Webb, E. K., Campbell, D. T., Schwartz, L., & Sechrest, L. (1966). *Unobtrusive measures: Nonreactive research in the social sciences.* Chicago: Rand McNally.

Webb, E. K., Campbell, D. T., Schwartz, L., Sechrest, L., & Grove, J. B. (1981). *Nonreactive measures in the social sciences.* Boston: Houghton Mifflin.

West, S. G., & Gunn, S. P. (1978). Some issues of ethics and social psychology. *American Psychologist, 33,* 30–38.

chapter 4

The Case Study Approach

Kathleen Manning

The purpose of a qualitative research case study is to evoke a description and interpretation of a culture. The case study can be used in student affairs to suggest a perspective from a student's point of view, furnish a slice of life about a college, and assess program goals. With their roots in sociology and anthropology, case studies have generally been used to describe cultures. Campus cultures have been shown to be an interesting and rich area of educational research (Horowitz, 1987; Kuh et al., 1991; Kuh & Whitt, 1988; Manning, 1990; Moffatt, 1989).

Case study research can portray a campus in depth in such a way that the reader gets a feel for what it was like to be there, to experience the campus as a student might, and to gain insight into the culture. The strengths of case studies are their depiction of a particular case, description of a specific context, and ability to provide an interpretive account of the way research participants make meaning. Case studies cannot be used to generalize to other cultures, provide evidence to prove a theory, or provide documentation of an intervention that can be transported as is to a different setting. The strength of case study research lies in the researcher's ability to conduct a study that is of high quality as well as ethically and methodologically sound.

This chapter discusses the history of the case study approach as well as techniques and methods of case study research (Bogdan & Biklen, 1982; Bulmer, 1984; Hammersley, 1989; Lincoln & Guba, 1985; Yin, 1984). These techniques include research design considerations, the

45

role of theory, explicating underlying assumptions, data collection and analysis, and case study writing. This chapter also provides suggestions and methods for researchers, administrators, and assessors to the case study approach and case studies. Writing the case study involves data analysis, conceiving insightful interpretations, and skillful writing. Specific steps to take when writing case studies are suggested.

HISTORY OF CASE STUDY APPROACH

The use of case studies and fieldwork as a research method began at the Chicago School of Sociology, University of Chicago, in the 1920s. Influenced by anthropology and journalism, Robert Parks conceptualized and routinized the practices of field research already in use by Chicago's sociology graduate students. Breaking from the tradition of sociological research of the time, Parks, in collaboration with Chicago colleague Ernest Burgess, determined that "detached and cynical observation from outside . . . was not enough. Real understanding also required imaginative participation in the lives of others, empathy as well as an acute eye" (Bulmer, 1984, p. 93). The emphasis was on the subjective experience of the social actor. Features of the Chicago case study approach included studies conducted by directly experiencing the "field," use of informal methods of interviewing and observation, labor-intensive and time-consuming methodology (e.g., the students "lived sociology"), and heavy influence by Parks and/or Burgess.

> A typical study would involve literature searches, the use of historical and current documentary materials, interviews with a wide variety of people, observation of relevant activities, and the collection of personal documents [usually life histories] from the subjects of the research, as well as the relevant statistical materials on ecological structure. (Bulmer, 1984, p. 100)

Case study research described in this chapter, though influenced by the Chicago School, differs from this historic approach to discovering knowledge. These differences include an interpretive approach, use of emergent paradigm assumptions (e.g., multiple perspectives, mutual interaction between researcher and respondents), and lack of generalizability of the findings to other contexts. The influence of the Chicago School, though, cannot be overstated.

RESEARCH DESIGN CONSIDERATIONS

The focus of the case study summarizes the aims and purposes of the research as well as raises questions to be explored through the research.

Unlike conventional methods of educational research, a hypothesis is not determined in advance. Rather, qualitative research begins with discovery and exploration typified by the question, "what's going on here?" (Lincoln & Guba, 1985). On campus the aim of the research could be to discover the meaning students hold for a campus tradition, assess the program goals of orientation, or discover students' opinions concerning the racial climate.

The focus draws boundaries around the research and keeps the research task manageable. A well-crafted and conceptualized focus assists the researcher to choose respondents from whom to collect data, analyze information in light of the assumptions of the focus, and make decisions and choices about data collection. The focus becomes clearer as the research proceeds and the researcher becomes more informed and knowledgeable about the issue under study. One of the researcher's responsibilities is to hone the focus and boundaries as the data collection and analysis proceed.

The boundaries that define the focus are conceptual, pragmatic, and logistical. Conceptual boundaries are the theories and disciplinary perspectives that inform the study. Pragmatic and logistic boundaries include time (e.g., duration of the study), place (e.g., setting for data collection), and financial support (e.g., research grant financing).

ROLE OF THEORY

Emergent paradigm research does not assume a theory-free or atheoretical stance. Theory gathered from a review of the existing literature can be used as a source of insights, ideas, and knowledge upon which to build a study. This theory, called *guiding theory*, provides an informed place from which to start the data collection and analysis. The educational researcher draws on social science theories (e.g., student development theory from psychology, cultural theory from anthropology, guiding principles of student affairs from history and philosophy) as well as practitioners' program theories and theories-in-use (Argyris, Putnam, & Smith, 1985; Greene, 1990; Stage, 1991) as a source for insights by which to guide the study. Guiding theory helps the researcher as he or she composes questions to ask respondents, sets boundaries for the focus, and builds interpretations from the data and with the respondents.

But guiding theory must be used carefully. Emergent paradigm research does not assume a priori categories or hypotheses; therefore, theory cannot be a source of conclusions determined in advance and proven through the research. Instead, as the researcher collects data he or she must listen carefully and open-mindedly to the knowledge being shared by the respondents and observed in the research setting. Rather than listening for what he or she found in the guiding theory, the researcher hears the knowledge shared by the respondent.

> Coming to understand a culture in a way even remotely similar to that of those that live within it is a continuous and, if the fieldworker is careful, a deepening interpretive process. Theoretical abstractions will not allow a fieldworker to get at the so-called heart of a culture any more quickly. (Van Maanen, 1988, p. 118)

Insights gleaned from guiding theory are used to inform the study without requiring that the researcher only "see" and "hear" knowledge congruent with the guiding theory.

UNDERLYING ASSUMPTIONS

Just as the researcher needs to take care that the beliefs and assumptions gleaned from theory do not overdirect the study, he or she must be equally cautious about other assumptions that impinge upon the study. Lincoln and Guba (1985) referred to a process called *value plurality* whereby the researcher makes explicit the underlying values or assumptions of the study. These values include those of the researcher, respondents, methodology, guiding theory, and research site. In order to take into account the multiple values that influence the study, the researcher can ask the following questions:

1. What are the underlying theoretical and methodological assumptions guiding the research (e.g., student involvement in cocurricular activities encourages retention)?
2. What are the underlying assumptions that characterize the respondents and the world in which they live (e.g., women's higher education mission of achievement and leadership)?
3. What personal characteristics (e.g., conservative politics, Latino heritage) influence the manner in which the researcher and respondents view the knowledge and issue under study?
4. What are the assumptions of the methodology guiding the study (e.g., student retention is a mutually shaping phenomenon of student and institutional characteristics)? How do those assumptions influence the study?

The point in this ongoing self-examination is to provide anyone who reads the case study with an idea of who the researcher was, how his or her assumptions influenced what was seen, how the beliefs at the re-

search site affected the data collection, and how the research methodology shaped the conceptual lens through which the researcher viewed
the data. An explanation of the values and assumptions of the site and
respondents can provide the case study reader with a context in which
to place the study.

A difficult question for the novice researcher is how to understand
his or her underlying assumptions as well as those of the respondents,
research site, guiding theory, and methodology. A fruitful place to start
is with the respondents. Listen closely to their words. Ask exploring
questions that disclose the meanings that underscore and inform their
words and the knowledge being shared. Do not take the respondents'
words for granted. Look for the deeper meaning of world view, cultural
perspective, and presumptions guiding their thinking and way of looking
at their experiences.

For example, there are points of view and assumptions that guide
action, behavior, and practice. The following sentences are examples of
underlying beliefs for student affairs practice:

- I trust people.
- The world is chaotic.
- Student development proceeds in sequential and orderly stages.
- I'm comfortable with my ethnicity.

These assumptions can be revealed in the case study by directly calling
the reader's attention to them. They can also be built into the case
study through use of language and terms that expose a set of theoretical
and conceptual assumptions. For example, the writer of the case study
exercises caution to be sure that the language he or she uses does not
include jargon alien to the reader and not inherent to the research site.
This language tends to distance the reader from the knowledge expressed in the case study.

DATA COLLECTION AND ANALYSIS

Data are collected primarily through interviews with respondents. (This
process is outlined in chapter 7.) Data are also collected through observation (e.g., campus activities, meetings) and document analysis (e.g.,
memos, yearbooks).

Data analysis, conducted as the data collection proceeds, is a process
of discovering the patterns and themes in the information shared by
the respondents (Lincoln & Guba, 1985). The analysis can be achieved
using computer programs designed specifically to aid transcription and

sorting. The method, unitizing and categorizing, described in this chapter relies on hand sorting.

The field notes are rewritten (or reformatted on a computer) onto 3″ by 5″ index cards. Each index card contains a complete quote, idea, or concept taken directly from the respondents or interpreted by the researcher. These "units" are sorted into categories (e.g., reasons for leaving school, cultural differences within the campus community) from which the study's themes emerge. These themes are the overarching, conceptual perceptions that point to the respondents' meaning. Examples of possible themes emerging from a retention study include presence of a supportive community, friendly feel of the campus, and presence of an academically challenging environment.

The simultaneous data collection and analysis enable the researcher to make decisions about additional information to be collected, the emerging interpretations, and refinements to the study's focus. These decisions and choices are not based on an external set of criteria but decided by the researcher in the context of the study's focus as well as the researcher's responsibility to the respondents.

Piles of cards sorted into categories are titled and built into themes that form the backbone of the study's findings. These themes are the theoretical and conceptual conclusions of the research. The process of building themes from the data is the most difficult aspect of qualitative research. There are no tricks to becoming more insightful about the deeper meanings within the respondents' words and actions. Questions for the researcher to raise toward this end are as follows:

1. What are the underlying assumptions that inform and guide the actions of the respondents? What does the respondent believe that leads him or her to say the words he or she does?
2. What are the phrases rich in meaning that the respondent has simply verbalized?
3. What's actually going on here? What does all this mean?
4. What are the beliefs and purposes of the community? How do these shape and influence the action observed and knowledge shared by the respondents?
5. What are the philosophical orientations of the respondents (e.g., feminist, Christian, conservative, egalitarian)? How does this give meaning to the actions and beliefs of the community?
6. What are the institutional structures (e.g., organizational configuration) and policies (e.g., community norms)? How do these enable and constrain participants? How do these influence the meaning made on individual and communal bases?

As the themes and interpretations emerge, they are reviewed by respondents through a process called *member checking* (Skrtic, 1985). Respondents edit and correct the field notes and draft themes to assure that the researcher's accounts are faithful to the meanings, feelings, and descriptions expressed by those respondents. Member checking assures that the themes and case study are co-constructed by the researcher and the respondents rather than interpreted only by the researcher.

Constructing themes in emergent paradigm research is different from the conventional paradigm process of generalizing. Generalizations (e.g., statements of prediction and control) extrapolate the meanings from the study to circumstances and contexts other than that of the research site. Generalizations depend on a representative sample and the belief that there is consistency and similarity across contexts. Building themes entails delving into the deeper meanings for the respondents, the researcher, and, eventually, the reader. Rather than taking the meanings to a location outside the data's context, themes remain embedded in the context of the research as expressed in the description and interpretation of the case study.

CASE STUDY WRITING

Six steps the researcher can take while writing the case study are suggested in this section. These steps involve choosing the information to include in the case study, compiling the interpretations, deciding the case study style, writing the first draft, and reviewing or member checking the nearly final draft with respondents.

Step 1: Decide What Data to Include

In the first step the researcher decides what data or information to include in the case study.

> Ethnographic writing of any kind is a complex matter, dependent on an uncountable number of strategic choices and active constructions (e.g., what details to include or omit; how to summarize and present data; what voice to select, what quotations to use). (Van Maanen, 1988, p. 73)

Qualitative research typically results in an overabundance of data. Not all data can or should be included in the case study. The goal is to avoid an all-inclusiveness or literal account of the respondents' words and, at the same time, produce a readable, emotionally evocative, narrative story conveying the findings and interpretations.

In fulfilling this first step the researcher can consider the following:

1. How do the data analyzed relate to the focus of the study?
2. Are the data interesting? Do they add to existing theory in the area under study?
3. What information can best convey the respondents' points of view and context of the study?
4. What information is complete enough to include in the case study?

The choices of data to leave out or to say incidentally can be as telling as those meanings that are stated explicitly and in detail. What is left out or *not* said can communicate as eloquently as those meanings conveyed candidly (Van Maanen, 1988).

Step 2: Compile the Themes

The second step when writing the case study is to compile the study's themes gleaned through data analysis. These themes, built throughout the simultaneous data collection and analysis processes, are organized, sorted into a cogent order, discarded as unimportant, and reworked into a readable form faithful to the knowledge shared by the respondents. These themes should emerge from the piles of cards sorted into categories.

Step 3: Decide Case Study Style

The third step in writing the case study is to decide the case study style. The number of styles available are as numerous as researchers in the field. Case studies in educational research are typically novel-like (e.g., highly descriptive and narrative) rather than formal (e.g., statistical charts with a constrained writing style).

The researcher can consider a variety of styles including a question-and-answer interview format, first-person life-histories, respondent quotes without the researcher's interpretations, narrative with thick description that tells a story, and a combination of guiding theory and research data synthesized into a report. In all cases, "make certain that your style reflects your intent in writing, the audience for whom the piece is intended, and most importantly, what you want to convey" (Bogdan & Biklen, 1982, p. 179).

A pivotal question in this decision about style is the researcher's perspective and voice. How does the researcher, primarily through the use of "I," locate him- or herself in the context of the research and literally in the case study? Does the researcher see him- or herself as the author (a solitary activity) or a coauthor (an activity conducted with respondents) of the case study? Will the case be written from the researcher's point of view or the native's point of view (Geertz, 1983)? Will an abstract theoretical point of view be assumed such that the case study is written from a discipline perspective (e.g., anthropological, educational, philosophical) or from an informal storytelling perspective?

Educational case studies are generally told from the respondents' points of view. If the researcher puts too much of him- or himself into the study, questions of oversubjectivity are immediately raised (Geertz, 1988). Too much of the researcher's voice could result in a lively tale about his or her experiences that makes interesting reading but is questionable in light of rigorous qualitative research standards.

Step 4: Write the First Draft

The fourth step is to write the first draft. Writing style is a personal decision, but an effective way to proceed is to arrange the categories or piles of cards into a coherent fashion, and then write the first draft of the case study progressing card by card until all piles are completed. The order of the piles of cards can be chronological by events observed, conceptual by patterns or themes, or in order by respondent case stories. Respondents' quotes, descriptions of events, and interpretations are incorporated into a running account that serves as the first draft of the case study. This first effort primarily is a descriptive one. The purpose is to "recreate . . . meaning with an appropriate image" (Bogdan & Biklen, 1982, p. 176).

Step 5: Rewrite and Edit Draft

The fifth step is to rewrite and edit the case study draft to build interpretations and thick description (Geertz, 1973) (i.e., evocative writing that conveys the physical, emotional, and philosophical beliefs of the setting). In the rewriting and editing the researcher concentrates efforts toward rich description, summarizes and expands interpretations, gains new insights into the data as they take form in the case study, and responds to respondents' comments and suggestions from their readings (i.e., member checking) of the drafts.

The rich description assists the reader to understand the respondents' meanings as well as vicariously experience the research site. The description should allow the reader to feel what it was like to be there

(Geertz, 1988). Thick description conveys the complexity of the respondents' lives.

The case study method described in this chapter arises from phenomenology (Bogdan & Biklen, 1982), critical theory (Giroux, 1988), and an interpretive approach to anthropology (Geertz, 1973, 1983, 1988). This perspective pushes research beyond description and encourages researchers to be insightful and interpretive about the data. This effort results in research that is theoretically sound, conceptually rich, and vigorously explanatory.

Interpretations, another prominent feature of the case study, can be directly inserted or, at other times, subtly implied. Interpretation of the case study data continues well after the case study is written. The reader uses personal history, experiences, and ways of understanding to gain and provide insights into the research. Readers build interpretations much as one interprets a poem. The case becomes a credible and powerful tool through which the reader evokes an image of the research context. These images include the sounds, sights, smells, and feelings of the research site and its people. This interpretive rendering of the case provides the research with its explanatory, conceptual, and theoretical depth. Qualitative research that is only descriptive has been justifiably criticized for being conceptually thin and theoretically meager (Glaser, 1978).

Step 6: Assure High Quality

The sixth and ongoing step is to assure that the study is of high quality and faithful to the words expressed by the respondents. A technique to assure this process is to have the nearly final case study member checked by several respondents. Care should be taken that those member checking the study understand that their corrections, additions, and suggestions are an essential part of the research analysis.

A high-quality case study can be further assured by having the case study audited (i.e., field notes and case study read by a methodologically informed but uninvolved peer). This final step provides information about the fit of the information shared in the case to the knowledge shared in the field notes (Lincoln & Guba, 1985, 1986; Skrtic, 1985).

Member checking is an important ethical obligation to assure coconstruction of the case study and conclusions. Other ethical considerations include sending a copy of the completed case study to the research site, using consent forms for all interviewing, being completely honest about the uses of the research, and fully explaining the focus of the study to all participants. This ethical practice enables the respondents to be fully informed and involved in the interpretations and conclusions generated through the study.

Although these suggestions for case study decisions are conveyed in a step-by-step manner, all decisions are ongoing. Description, interpretation, data collection, and data analysis are continuous and simultaneous processes. Even as the case study is being written, interpretations are rethought and decisions remade about the descriptive and interpretive salience of the data.

CONCLUSION

A case study is not simply a chronicle of the events, circumstances, and respondents' impressions of the college under study. It is a text with a structure and organization. This structure is a tool crafted and used to convey the knowledge and meanings expressed by the respondents. The structure, form, style, and voice of the case study are ways to express the content and knowledge of the culture.

The case study can be used in student affairs research and assessment as a way to explain the complexity of colleges and universities. Through these cases practitioners gain an understanding of the meanings that students, administrators, and faculty hold about those communities.

FURTHER READING

Eisner, E., & Peshkin, A. (1990). *Qualitative inquiry in education: The continuing debate*. New York: Teachers College Press.

Goetz, J., & LeCompte, M. (1984). *Ethnography and qualitative design in educational research*. New York: Academic Press.

Guba, E. (Ed.). (1990). *The paradigm dialog*. Beverly Hills, CA: Sage.

Hammersley, M., & Atkinson, P. (1983). *Ethnography: Principles in practice*. New York: Routledge.

Kuhn, T. (1962). *The structure of scientific revolutions* (2nd ed.). Chicago: University of Chicago Press.

Lincoln, Y. (Ed.). (1985). *Organizational theory and inquiry: The paradigm revolution*. Beverly Hills, CA: Sage.

Taylor S., & Bogdan, R. (1984). *Introduction to qualitative research methods: The search for meanings* (2nd ed.). New York: Wiley.

Van Maanen, J. (Ed.). (1979). *Qualitative methodology*. Beverly Hills, CA: Sage.

Wolcott, H. (1990). *Writing up qualitative research*. Newbury Park, CA: Sage.

REFERENCES

Argyris, C., Putnam, R., & Smith, D. (1985). *Action science.* San Francisco: Jossey-Bass.

Bogdan, R., & Biklen, S. (1982). *Qualitative research for education: An introduction to theory and methods.* Boston: Allyn and Bacon.

Bulmer, M. (1984). *The Chicago School of Sociology: Institutionalization, diversity, and the rise of sociological research.* Chicago: University of Chicago Press.

Geertz, C. (1973). Thick description: Toward an interpretive theory of culture. In C. Geertz (Ed.), *The interpretation of cultures* (pp. 37–59). New York: Basic Books.

Geertz, C. (1983). *Local knowledge.* New York: Basic Books.

Geertz, C. (1988). *Works and lives: The anthropologist as author.* Stanford, CA: Stanford University Press.

Giroux, H. (1988). *Schooling and the struggle for public life.* Minneapolis: University of Minnesota Press.

Glaser, B. (1978). *Theoretical sensitivity.* San Francisco: University of California Press.

Greene, J. (1990, April). *The nature and role of theory in qualitative program evaluation.* Paper presented at the meeting of the American Educational Research Association, Boston.

Hammersley, M. (1989). *The dilemma of qualitative method: Herbert Blumer and the Chicago tradition.* New York: Routledge.

Horowitz, H. (1987). *Campus life: Undergraduate cultures from the end of the 18th century to the present.* Chicago: University of Chicago Press.

Kuh, G., Schuh, J., Whitt, E., Andreas, R., Lyons, J., Strange, C., Krehbiel, L., & MacKay, K. (1991). *Involving colleges: Successful approaches to fostering student learning and development outside the classroom.* San Francisco: Jossey-Bass.

Kuh, G., & Whitt, E. (1988). *The invisible tapestry: Culture in American colleges and universities.* Washington, DC: ASHE-ERIC Higher Education Reports (No. 1).

Lincoln, Y., & Guba, E. (1985). *Naturalistic inquiry.* Beverly Hills, CA: Sage.

Lincoln, Y., & Guba, E. (1986). But is it rigorous? Trustworthiness and authenticity in naturalistic evaluation. In D. Williams (Ed.), *Naturalistic evaluation* (pp. 73–84). San Francisco: Jossey-Bass.

Manning, K. (1990). *Campus rituals and cultural meaning.* Unpublished doctoral dissertation, Indiana University, Bloomington.

Moffatt, M. (1989). *Coming of age in New Jersey.* New Brunswick, NJ: Rutgers University Press.

Skrtic, T. (1985). Doing naturalistic research into educational organizations. In Y. Lincoln (Ed.), *Organizational theory and inquiry: The paradigm revolution.* (pp. 185–220). Beverly Hills, CA: Sage.

Stage, F. (1991). Common elements of theory: A framework for college student development. *Journal of College Student Development, 31*(1), 56–61.

Van Maanen, J. (1988). *Tales of the field: On writing ethnography.* Chicago: University of Chicago Press.

Yin, R. (1984). *Case study research design and methods.* Beverly Hills, CA: Sage.

chapter 5

The Use of Historical Methods

Robert A. Schwartz

For many people history conjures up memories of high school examinations replete with multiple-choice questions on old dates, faraway wars, and dead kings. This is an unfortunate and mistaken image. History and historical analysis need not be a boring, uninspired recitation of facts. The use of historical methods and analysis in higher education, in particular when used to assess or investigate students in higher education, can be helpful, enlightening, and even exciting.

This chapter provides an overview of the use of historical methods in research and assessment of college students. Specific reasons for the use of a historical approach as well as concrete examples are offered. The primary purpose of this chapter is to give an introduction to the use of the historical method in conducting assessments of or research on college students. Information on terminology, method, and applications for the historical method are presented. Examples of the use of history to examine higher education and college students are given throughout the chapter, and suggestions for further reading and sources of information are in the final section.

WHY USE HISTORICAL METHODS?

Using historical methods for campus assessment or research can be extremely beneficial. The historical approach can be applied to such diverse questions as "Has the student population changed over the last

25 or 50 years?'' and ''How has the curriculum evolved on this particular campus?'' Historical methods in education can and have been used to study ethnic groups, women, the family, institutions, policies, curricula, and social reform movements. In many respects, the use of history to study higher education is limited only by our imagination.

James Rhatigan (1978), vice-president for student affairs at Wichita State, has observed that:

> few [student affairs] administrators see the relevance or importance of historical forces and issues to the present status. . . . This is a grievous miscalculation. History provides perspective and without an understanding [of the past] . . . we have a truncated knowledge of our profession in particular and of campus development in general. In our field, the present is a dominant preoccupation. (p. 9)

In support of Rhatigan's assertion, consider the following historical tidbits. Fraternities were once thought to be radical groups that threatened campus stability (DiMartini, 1974). Female students constituted such a large proportion of the college student population in the early 20th century that they clearly intimidated male faculty and male students, in large part because they proved to be very capable students (Graham, 1978). African-American women learned to read by lip reading and mimicking the White children they cared for in plantation homes; they then taught this important, and liberating, skill to their families (Jones, 1985). United States domestic and foreign policy in the 20th century was strongly influenced by 16 headmasters at elite prep schools in the Northeast (Saveth, 1988). These are not just curiosities but important realities, critical to the accurate interpretation of American educational history.

As Hodgkinson (1985) asserted, education *is* ''all one system.'' In the same sense, contemporary education *is* the product of a system of education that extends from colonial times to the present. It is a cumulative history that encompasses the education of small children as well as graduate students and professional schools. To ignore the information that can be revealed through a lens of historical inquiry is, at best, unfortunate and unnecessary.

There are many decision makers who, although concerned with access to education for Black students, have no idea what the Atlanta Compromise was, much less why Booker T. Washington proposed it, nor what the debate it engendered with W.E.B. DuBois was about (Harlan, 1972). Although the number of women students now exceeds the number of men on most campuses, few administrators are aware that in the first half of the 20th century, women accounted for nearly half (47%) of all undergraduate college students (Solomon, 1985). Armed with such knowledge, it is the *de*crease in female students from the late 1940s to the mid-1960s that appears to be the exception, not the *in*crease that appears in the 1970s. Long before the *Student Personnel Point of View* was published in 1937, deans of women had already organized the first professional student affairs organizations (1903), collected and published research (1910), and written the first book in student affairs—*The Dean of Women* (1915), by Lois K. Mathews, dean of women at the University of Wisconsin (Schwartz, 1990). Obviously, these events had a strong bearing on the nature of the profession and still do today. Unfortunately, knowledge voids such as these limit higher education policy and decision making. They can also be embarrassing omissions in our personal professional knowledge base. It is imperative that members of the higher education and student affairs fields make better use of educational history, historical research, and historical interpretation.

In a course designed for government policy makers at Harvard, Neustadt and May (1986) taught their students how to use history to make better decisions. Neustadt and May suggested that history can be used to examine current situations by examining "likenesses and differences" between current and past events as well as by looking at "the known," "the unclear," and "the presumed." Through history, we can learn to ask "What's the story?" and begin to unravel the real from the perceived and the known from the unknown.

Thinking in time, as Neustadt and May (1986) suggested, is really thinking historically. As we become more aware of history, we begin to see that the present and the future are a part of a stream of events that have their roots in the past. Given this new perspective, we understand human endeavor more completely and more clearly. A similar use of history to influence decisions and policy in higher education administration can be equally valuable.

Learning more about a particular event, development, policy, or institution through historical study should be exciting as well as empowering. Historical analysis can establish a solid base of knowledge from which to analyze and interpret contemporary events. Indeed, much of what we depend upon in American culture and society is based on precedent and prior actions (Neustadt & May, 1986). As a result, those willing to study developments historically can shape new or different interpretations of events and developments. As Robert Jones Shafer (1980) put it, "Historical literature has its greatest function as an addition to individual experience, giving to the single human being an understanding that men and women many times in the history of the race have confronted similar problems."

The Civil War has often been portrayed in school history as a war fought over the emancipation of slaves; it was just as much, if not more, a pitched battle over the economic future of the United States (Robertson, 1980). The industrial, urbanized states of the North had a much different agenda for the future growth of the country than did the agrarian, rural states of the South. In another example, consider how differently the history of the war in Vietnam might be perceived from the point of view of a North Vietnamese writer as opposed to a politically conservative American.

We tend to assume, erroneously, that history speaks with a single voice. In fact, there are many voices. This perspective is especially true in American higher education and in the assessment of students and student cultures within higher education. Female college students, for example, perceive, think, and feel differently about their collegiate experience than do male college students (Belenky, Clinchy, Goldberger, & Tarule, 1986; Gilligan, 1982). Consequently, women may have a much different history of reactions, perceptions, and feelings about their collegiate experience than do men, as Antler (1987), Fass (1977), Graham (1978), Horowitz (1986, 1987), and others have demonstrated. The same is true for other groups whose experiences differ from the traditions of White, male, middle-class America. Even the prevailing notions about the growth of the American system of higher education have been challenged by historical revisions, such as Bledstein's (1978) reinterpretation of the response of middle-class Americans to the "promise" of higher education or recent institutional studies of higher education such as Lawrence Veysey's *The Emergence of the American University* (1965).

History can take many forms. Carl Kaestle (1988), speaking about the history of education has said, "There is no single, definable method of inquiry, and important historical generalizations are rarely beyond dispute. . . . History is a challenging and creative interaction, part science, part art" (p. 67). In the same vein, Neustadt and May (1986) encouraged their students at Harvard to see time "as a stream" and "to imagine the future as it may be when it becomes the past." Similar measures can prove useful for campus policy makers, student affairs practitioners, and researchers interested in college students. At the very least, historical analysis brings an increased awareness of the past as well as fresh interpretations of the present and the future.

Advantages

A historical analysis can be user friendly in that it does not require numerical data analysis (although many good historical studies do use quantitative methods). A historical approach can yield tremendous gains in understanding a concern or issue. New interpretations of past events are often the best guides to new approaches or alternative policies. On a more personal level, the use of historical inquiry and analysis can give us a sense of confidence and knowledge that comes only from an increased familiarity with the lessons of the past.

A literature review, an early and important step in historical analysis, is often critical to any research effort, so the time invested as a part of a historical analysis is never a wasted effort. In fact, it may be quite useful even if another alternative method is eventually selected instead. And further, the tedium of a literature review has been greatly eased by technology, such as the electronic databases that can quickly sort through existing sources.

Disadvantages

The fact that a thorough literature search requires a commitment of time and effort is inescapable. To those researchers for whom time is a critical issue, it may be that the necessity of a broad and thorough literature search, an unavoidable necessity, may preclude the use of the historical method. A warning specific to the "math anxious": The time required to complete a thorough historical study may easily exceed any advantage gained by avoiding the "number-crunching" of a statistical analysis. The quick fix and the use of historical analysis are *not* complementary approaches. Some other disadvantages that may be encountered when using historical analysis may involve the availability of sources (although interlibrary loan and the technological databases currently in use ameliorate this problem to a large degree), the applicability of history to a particular concern, the urgency for the information and analysis, and the ability to convince others that a historical methodology is appropriate.

TERMINOLOGY

The terminology of historical inquiry in education is not difficult. It is important to know, however, that the histories of education, like individuals in a group, are not all the same. Just as there are a variety of statistical tests that can be applied to a particular research problem, so can any number of historical approaches or applications be used to examine the universe of education history. Terms are defined in this section, specifically *primary and secondary sources* and *internal and external criticism.*

For the most part, historical analysis does not require the learning of complex formulas or sophisticated computer skills. It does, however, call for a critical eye in interpreting and analyzing information and data as well as persistence, determination, and a creative and imaginative approach to thinking about the research.

Primary and Secondary Sources

The terminology of historical inquiry includes the terms *primary* and *secondary* to refer to sources of historical information. Primary sources are those documents or other accounts of an event or activity that are told or related from the perspective of someone who actually witnessed the occurrence. Secondary sources, as the name implies, are those accounts that are secondhand or are interpretations of another individual's primary account. In many cases, historians will give preference to the primary source as the most reliable, although even a primary source may be biased or distorted due to any number of conditions. In the same manner, a secondary source can be quite accurate and even improve on a primary source through amalgamation of different perspectives.

Historical data typically are collected from a variety of sources. Sources of history can be found in existing documents, for example, letters, statistical records, books, photographs, notes, and minutes of meetings. The term can also be extended to include audio and video tape and other recorded information. Newspapers and diaries can be sources of significant information for historical analysis and interpretation, as are buildings and other structures. Such an architectural history study might be quite useful, especially if directly related to issues such as student residence, student union buildings, or other common areas, not to mention the classroom. A very significant arena for historical data collection is taking oral histories from persons who witnessed certain events or tracking such information through stories, legends, and similar methods of passing on information orally. This is especially important for study of those groups or cultures in which reading and writing were not available or common, such as African-American slaves. In essence, historical research can be done using a wide variety of sources and is not limited to only written records.

External and Internal Criticism

Two other terms that may be encountered are *external* and *internal* in reference to criticism. Shafer (1980) has noted that many historians seldom engage in external criticism, a procedure to authenticate a source and guard against forgery or an illegitimate piece of evidence. It is not likely that this will be a major concern in the assessment of students. Internal criticism is concerned with the validity of an interpretation made by a researcher analyzing a set of historical information.

In other words, to what degree does the analysis hold up given the sources of information used? Internal criticism takes into account the intent and purpose of the source or original recorder of the event, the context in which the information was reported or written, and supporting evidence. For more information, see Shafer (1980) or Sherman and Kirshner (1976), among others. For the present discussion, it is sufficient to note the major areas of evaluation. For example, How does the source describe the event? Could the source be prejudiced towards one side or the other? Was the source actually present during the event (primary) or is this a case of someone reporting on an event after the fact (secondary)? How much is the source's point of view corroborated by other witnesses or documentation? Does this description make sense, given other information you have uncovered? Asking such questions and applying them to sources of information in a common sense manner is a good beginning to solid internal criticism.

THE USE OF HISTORICAL RESEARCH

Existing articles and books can serve as rich sources of information for those not yet familiar with the historical method in education. *Reading* historical studies is excellent preparation for *doing* historical research in education and should help to generate questions and avenues for further research. The rich writing, critical analysis, and variety of interpretations offered by much of the existing historical research in education provide a fertile training ground for the researcher new to the field. The final section of this chapter identifies some specific examples.

The Research Question

One of the most critical aspects of any research is posing the question that guides the research effort. If the question is clear, focused, and pertinent, it can give the researcher a beacon to follow throughout the entire endeavor. However, the research question often is composed of a patchwork of smaller questions. These smaller questions may be framed from a variety of sources, such as an anomaly unanswered by available information, a nagging discrepancy that has never been resolved, or, in some cases, a task assigned or assumed by virtue of the researcher's position, such as policy planner, institutional researcher, or student affairs officer.

In any case, it matters little where the research question came from or its original inspiration. What is critical is that the research question is something that can be investigated. As such, it is important that the focus of the initial research be narrow and deliberate. Typically, the very early research effort will be to identify related or preferably directly connected information in the area. Especially noteworthy are existing studies in the same area. In short, a good review of the literature is a necessity.

As an example of this process, let us hypothesize that a group of administrators and faculty are interested in determining the feasibility of adding a program in business to an existing campus curriculum with the intention of developing a school of business over the next decade. Obviously, this proposition will require a significant amount of preparation and planning, not the least of which could (and should be) the use of some historical research. Sound historical research on students should be a significant branch, if not the primary focus, of the research that leads to such a curricular and policy change. This information will help the planners document and either justify a major change or perhaps avoid an ill-conceived calamity if the research shows that this effort is unwarranted based on past events and experiences. In addition, actual historical analysis of institutional as well as state and federal educational policy should be illustrative as well (Warren, 1983), as could a review of the history of curriculum (Kliebard & Franklin, 1983).

In this case, the research question already has been framed by the proposed addition to the curriculum and ultimately to the mission of the college. As such, the question—How will a program in business change the nature of the institution and the population of students, both current and in the future, of this institution?—becomes the focus of the research effort. Several possibilities come to mind in terms of research or analysis that could prove helpful in this situation. One approach simply could be to explore the development of schools of business in the United States, or within the particular geographic region of the country where the institution in question is located. Another approach could be to consider the number of other programs in business in the same region and the populations of students involved over time in business studies at those institutions.

These initial ventures may well turn up other questions or considerations that have not yet been considered by the researcher(s) or others interested in the project. It may be that students have pursued degrees in other professional schools in a particular region for a long period of time. Such information, which is readily available in the *Digest of Education Statistics* or similar collections, could be critical to the proposed policy decisions.

What might such information reveal? Could it disclose trends, developments, and significant changes in the ebb and flow of prospective students over time? Could the information be examined further in terms of gender, degree earned, and geographic preference? Will it make a difference to the researcher and to the institution that over the previous three to four decades students chose to pursue certain professional degrees over others at some institutions? Will it make a difference that these students, in choosing, did not pursue other degrees or other schools? Even if it does not make a difference, most administrators and faculty would prefer knowing about such distinctions before making final decisions about the program.

Another research perspective could be to pursue information on the nature and historical antecedents of the professional degree in business. For example, in pondering such decisions, are the institution and its decision makers aware of the history of business degrees, such as Schmotter's (1990) history of the MBA at Cornell? When did the degree first come into existence and why? Has the MBA become prominent recently or has there always been credibility associated with additional education and graduate degrees in the business world? Are there significant national as well as regional trends to be considered? At what point does a program gain credibility? After 5 years? After 10? After 20? What is the institutional history with regard to the addition of new programs? Are there other institutions in the area that have had similar experiences over time? What is their past record? It may be important to move from national historical trends and broad histories to the region in question and, finally, to the specific institution. All of these questions are more readily answered through historical research and analysis than any other method of interpretation and analysis.

SPECIFICS FOR THE RESEARCHER

What to Do

A necessary feature of "conducting" historical research is access to a substantial amount of information or sources, both primary and secondary. For the researcher or practitioner concerned with research on students, the immediate campus can be a ready contributor of such information, especially as most campuses have a library, archives, and, often as not, other less obvious repositories of information, such as student artifacts, institutional records concerning students and student life, and the collective memories of faculty and alumni.

The Early Search

For most historical researchers, the standard note card is an indispensable tool. The cards are used to record brief notes on bibliographic material during the literature search. Brief notations recorded on cards are an invaluable means of collecting the pieces of information needed for sound historical analysis. The preference for note cards is rooted in practicality and experience because the method is simple yet allows for the constant rearrangement and reconsideration of a great deal of information over time (Shafer, 1980). (Even in conducting research by gathering oral histories, note cards combined with tape recorded data are an efficient means of organizing and reorganizing material into new categories easily.)

Armed with a set of new 3″ by 5″, 4″ by 6″, or other preferred size of note cards, the erstwhile historical researcher heads for the library, or university archives, or local museum to conduct the early search. In essence, the research to be completed at this point is a broad-reaching investigation of the research question. By scanning the card catalog and other research collections, including electronic databases and government documents, a focus for further research should begin to emerge. At this stage, the process is one of detective work, locating clues or possibilities for more in-depth research by looking globally in the area of interest. Although it is impossible to avoid the frustration of following several research dead ends, even finding nothing can be helpful if only because the search has been diminished.

As an example, if a researcher is interested in the pursuit of information about the growth of the social fraternity on the college campus in the 20th century, he or she might examine the card catalog under a wide variety of topics, including "fraternity," "college fraternity," or "student organizations." The use of similar descriptors could be applied to electronic databases, such as the ERIC Silver Platter, Dissertation Abstracts, and others. Additionally, in looking at existing historical treatments, the researcher might look for books on student life and cultures, or journals such as the *History of Education Quarterly.* Books that might prove helpful could include histories of individual fraternities or larger studies, for example, Helen Horowitz's *Campus Life: Undergraduate Cultures from the 19th Century to the Present* (1987).

In scanning Horowitz's book, the vigilant researcher might see a footnote in a chapter on early student organizations on campuses. The footnote refers, very positively, to a larger study conducted by DiMartini (1974) on the influence of fraternities at the University of Illinois in the 1800s. Intrigued, the researcher notes on a card the pertinent information from the Horowitz book and the original source of the DiMartini article: the *Journal of Social History,* volume 9, pages 526–541. As a result of this effort, two potentially excellent sources of information have been discovered.

Seeking out the *Journal of Social History,* the researcher finds DiMartini's article entitled "Student Culture as a Change Agent in American Higher Education: An Example From the 19th Century." The article describes how social fraternities, banned by presidential edict from the University of Illinois from its early years in the 1870s, persisted as *sub rosa* student organizations. In fact, the thesis of the author is that the social fraternities held such power in terms of influencing student opinion and reaction to institutional policy that they forced significant changes on the University of Illinois campus, including the elimination of the hated compulsory military drill.

This interpretation of events on the University of Illinois campus gives a new and unexpected dimension to the current research effort underway. In light of this article, it is possible to consider social fraternities, at least historically, as cultural change agents on the college campus. In making such an assessment, however, it is necessary to ask critical questions about these conclusions. Do other examples exist beyond the University of Illinois, or was this a unique situation? How well does DiMartini support his argument? What are *his* sources? Is this information worth pursuing? Or is it better left as "interesting but not relevant" on the note card(s)? These are typical questions that can be expected in the early historical research effort.

Starts and stops as just described can be collected on bibliographic note cards and then shuffled and rearranged to suit the focus of the research. As Shafer (1980) suggested, a regular and consistent format reaps huge dividends in the end. For example, the researcher must be sure to include not only author, title, and year but also the physical location of the source. In the written notes, the researcher must make critical decisions about the collected information, such as the value, topical area, or relevance of the source, the main theme of the article or research, and so forth. A numerical rank—or even a letter grade—can be used, such as 1 through 10 or A, B, C, such that a 10 or an A denotes higher quality or potential than does a 7 or a B. As a result, when the information is reviewed later during the analysis and integration process, choices can be made about use of material. It is important to remember that time invested during the first note-taking process will be invaluable later. Nothing is more frustrating than to have to return to the same source unnecessarily, a problem that becomes even more significant when travel or other mitigating factors such as deadlines or memory loss enter in.

An interesting sidelight to the pursuit of historical research, the evolving research question, may be inferred from the preceding example. As the investigation continues, the researcher might find that the original question has begun to change or evolve. The more one learns, the greater the temptation to spend greater and greater amounts of time pursuing a variety of avenues of research. What may have at first appeared to be a clear, discernible research question can become a murky pond of diverse possibilities. This is a good checkpoint. If there is a lot of material to consider, it means that the research has been fruitful and worthwhile. However, it probably means there also are far too many different avenues to pursue effectively. It is imperative at this point to sort out what the ongoing focus of the research should be. It may be important to go back to the original question for reexamination. Does it still make sense in light of all you know now? Does the question need to be changed? Can you make slight adjustments without losing sight of the original goal? In sorting out the possibilities, it can be very helpful to discuss the research with another person who is familiar with the general area of interest or at least with the intent of the research.

Above all else, take heart. Remember, it is important to know a great deal to conduct good historical research; in fact, "you will probably know a lot more than you can write" (W. Reese, personal communication, December 1989). In one sense, the historical researcher must serve two roles: the investigator who uncovers the information and the critic who examines the direction and flow of the information and challenges the same data set. Although this process is not easy, it is well worth the effort.

Along with the issues discussed so far, each piece of information considered must be subjected to some level of internal criticism as a check on reliability and validity. Shafer (1980) and Barzun and Graff (1962), among others, offered helpful checklists and guides for the novice to use in assessing the quality of evidence. In particular, the researcher must pay close attention to the circumstances under which the author of a piece of information observed a particular incident, the author's ability to report, as well as his or her intent in reporting such information. Shafer also called attention to concerns such as internal contradictions and the researcher's level of confidence after reading an account of an event. It is important to remember that the quality of the final research report or essay will only be as good as the accuracy and authenticity of the assembled pieces of historical evidence.

Later Stages

As the research effort progresses, the assembled information should begin to gain a critical mass. At this point, the research begins to turn from collection to assessment, analysis, synthesis, and interpretation.

One of the first steps to be taken at this point is to consider how well the collected information works as a whole. Do the pieces fit together? Does any of the evidence conflict with the whole or do any of the parts contradict each other? Why? In assembling the various parts of the mosaic, the foremost concern becomes Does the information presented corroborate itself? Ideally, the pieces should support each other after each has been tested through vigorous independent analysis. As a whole, or parts of a whole, the pieces should not only fit but support each other. In the previous example, does the information about fraternities at the University of Illinois fit with an overall picture of the growth of fraternities nationally? Did students really belong to fraternities and risk expulsion from a college or university as a means of resisting the power of college administrators? Could such student groups really have changed the campus culture as DiMartini (1974) suggested? How long did this rebellion go on? Did these early events affect fraternity membership? In what ways?

In considering these questions, the researcher may discover that many college administrators in the early 1900s had been members of fraternities. Thus college presidents and administrators, such as deans of men, were often fraternity alumni, a fact that would support the growth of the fraternity (Schwartz, 1990). In fact, deans of men in the early to mid-20th century praised the fraternity as a means of cultural and social control for male students, who, by virtue of their fraternity membership, were held to strict social and cultural standards by their peers (Clark, 1914; Finnegan, 1990). However, corroboration such as this is gained only through additional research.

Analysis and Synthesis

At this point, the information collected comes to the analysis and synthesis phase of the research effort. The enterprising researcher is urged to consult Shafer (1980), Barzun and Graff (1962), and others directly for complete information about this phase; but some brief suggestions follow.

The initial bibliographic research should provide a reasonable level of support for the original or, more likely, amended hypotheses. At this point, it should be possible to begin to combine, compare, and select the information in a meaningful manner. This is the process of analysis and synthesis (Shafer, 1980). Certain information that has been collected should corroborate other pieces, and a more complete picture should begin to emerge. The research note cards may even be arranged physically, if helpful, in chronological or thematic order on a table or even the floor. It can be helpful to rough out an outline or a timeline of events, activities, people, and so on. These visual aids can ease the difficulty of trying to arrange and rearrange the visual images in one's head as new interpretations come to mind. It also may be helpful to try and describe to another person (or even to a tape recorder) different arrangements or connections. The state of electronic word processing may be a real boon to this process, but it is not without complications. Although sorting information by computer is a useful endeavor, in historical analysis the most useful tool for analysis and synthesis is located between the researcher's ears.

Shafer (1980) offered an outline of the 15 elements necessary for the complete process of synthesis in historical writing. These include the following:

1. [determining] literal and real meaning; observation and reporting of detail
2. [sorting out] bias and subjectivity
3. [making sure of] corroboration, contradiction, and measurement; plausibility; probability and certainty
4. creating and using the working hypothesis; causation; [in short, does it make sense?]
5. motivation [how did this come about?]
6. individuals and institutions; contingency [why?]
7. [what else could have been at work?]; facts as values, ideas, and objects
8. inference; relevance; and arrangement [whose interpretation? and how to present the interpretation?].*

As a draft emerges, the researcher/author will want to reconsider what Kaestle (1988) called the "four fundamental methodological concerns" in historical analysis. These include:

> (1) the confusion of correlations and causes . . . [in which] . . . causality is about how things work, and correlations don't tell us much about how things work; (2) the distinction between evidence of ideas about how people **should** behave, and evidence of how ordinary people **in fact** behaved . . . [or] we assume people did as they were told; (3) the distinction between intent and consequences . . . assuming that the historical actors could have (and **should** have) foreseen the full consequences of their ideas and the institutions they shaped; and (4) defining key terms . . . [especially] . . . vagueness and presentism. (pp. 68–70)

---

*From *A Guide to the Historical Method* (pp. 194–195) by R. J. Shafer © 1980. Chicago: Dorsey/Wadsworth. Used by permission.

Vagueness, as it sounds, is using broad, umbrella terms, such as *industrialization* that defy specificity, and *presentism* is "the danger of assuming terms had their present-day connotations in the past" (p. 68).

As Kaestle (1988) further observed,

> no historian can completely transcend or resolve the four problems, but each must recognize the problems and the associated methodological challenges when trying to make meaningful generalizations about our educational past and to sort out the tremendous array of diverse and conflicting views that are presently circulating. (pp. 70–71)

Such admonitions could be categorized under the heading of "further internal criticism," but these particular concerns deserve separate attention.

The careful researcher in any discipline needs to be cautious about generalizations and assumptions while simultaneously asserting some well-defined conclusions and interpretations. This is the case as well with historical analysis and interpretation. Unlike quantitative studies (which can and do have a significant place in historical research), there is not a statistical level of significance that can be used to dismiss or confirm a historical interpretation. Rather, it is the responsibility of the primary author to critique the work for flaws or unfounded conclusions. It can be helpful to have an outside person review work in progress or final drafts for omissions, errors, or logical flaws. It also is important to compare our efforts to other interpretations in the same area. Although it is acceptable to have a conflicting or divergent interpretation, the justification for such differences must be able to withstand the rigor of scholarly criticism and comparison to prevailing ideas.

As a clearer picture begins to emerge, initial drafts of actual writing can be completed. Depending on the scope of the end result, it is advisable to write in short bursts and focus on one area at a time. If there are natural breaks, such as decades, groups, institutions, or the like, it may be easiest to concentrate on one at a time. Word processing equipment can be very helpful to the writer completing a historical analysis, as notes that apply to later or earlier chapters or periods can be added at will. It is possible and even desirable that more analysis and synthesis will occur as the writing unfolds, so often the challenge is to keep writing, to tell the story without immediate concern for revision.

Reporting Results of the Study

As drafts of the writing are produced, the researcher should make corrections in presentation as well as in the synthesis and analysis of the information. Good writing is critical to good historical interpretation, so every effort must be made to ensure that the meaning of a piece is clear and that the work reads well as a written piece and a history. It is also not unusual to find that revisions enlarge an early work as it evolves over time. Additional efforts on the part of the author to be clear and coherent and yet rethink the interpretation may expand or condense the early drafts.

As the pieces begin to fit together under the original or amended research question, the other issue becomes how to present the information in such a way that it can be both informative and scholarly. In other words, How can the findings be presented to others so that they are interesting and valid? In part, this is a question of good writing and will be left for others to discuss. However, it is also a question of organization and presentation, which are pertinent to the present discussion.

Several points about organization should be considered. Perhaps the easiest means of organizing a historical study is to use chronological order, in essence taking things in the order in which they occurred and retelling the story. In this way, the assembly is by date(s), starting with the earliest and working forward to the present or latest. However, this may not always tell the story accurately or provide the analytic interpretation that is appropriate or relevant. Other means include topical or even geographical organization (Shafer, 1980). These are by no means conclusive; the researcher must find the most appropriate means of broadly categorizing or organizing information themes.

It has been suggested that using historical research or even reading historical studies can empower the researcher or the reader in ways that are difficult to replicate with other research methods. In higher education especially, the tendency of much of the research is to focus on the present or to speculate on the future. Rarely are researchers, administrators, and policy makers concerned with what happened in the past. It seems as though the older the thing, body, or event becomes, the less significance it has (Rhatigan, 1978).

However, those persons who can link past events, trends, behaviors, policies, and persons to patterns, cycles, and epochs are often respected, admired, and occasionally revered for their insight and wisdom. An awareness and knowledge of history make it easier to see forests where others may see only trees. Gaining historical knowledge requires a level of commitment and discipline to use history as a tool for either research or personal edification.

CONCLUSION

The most critical aspect of using historical research or assessment is to plunge in and give it a try. The historical method can be most useful, enlightening, and applied to almost any research or assessment issue. Individually, the greatest benefit to be gained is the discovery of an interpretive lens through which events and actions can be seen as a part of a continuum rather than as single, isolated bursts of activity; the process is analogous to viewing a movie as opposed to looking at a single photograph. Institutionally, as well as in policy formulation, frequent use of historical interpretation and analysis can reveal similarities and analogies to the present and even help anticipate the future (Neustadt & May, 1986). Historical research methods can be a rich source of information and knowledge, much of which is close at hand and accessible. The challenge is to tap the sources and put this valuable research method to good use in a consistent manner.

Although this chapter has attempted to persuade the reader of the value of the historical method in assessment and research, the very best advice is to be multifaceted. Shulman (1988) suggested that anyone interested in conducting good research and assessment in education needs to "attempt to become skilled and experienced in at least two forms of research methodology. Facility in only one strikes me as somewhat dangerous, the equivalent of a methodological 'Johnny One-Note' " (p. 16).

FURTHER READING

It is tempting, at this juncture, to recommend far too many resources at the risk of omitting something truly significant. As stated earlier, one of the very best ways to become familiar with the use of history as an analytic and interpretive tool in higher education is to read voraciously. On the other hand, if there is only time for one good book on the topic, John Thelin's *Higher Education and Its Useful Past: Applied History in Research and Planning* (1982) is the best choice. It covers all of the above material, only better. (For specific publication data for this and other publications mentioned in this section, see the reference list that follows.)

An excellent beginning point for most researchers and practitioners alike is to seek out an institutional history for the college or university where they are presently employed. Other options include a history of our undergraduate or graduate school, or any other institution of choice. There is a wide range of institutional histories to draw upon, and some are excellent.

It may be especially important for those in higher education to increase their awareness of American education in general, as higher education has often been rather ethnocentric. Seeing education as all one system historically as well as demographically can be invaluable; after all, those new freshmen students experienced at least 12 years of prior schooling somewhere! Several good overviews of American education include authors as diverse and interesting as Lawrence Cremin, Ellwood Cubberly, Joel Spring, Michael Katz, and Robert Church and Michael Sedlak. Edward Krug, who specialized in the history of the American high school, are worth serious consideration as well. Journals, such as the *History of Education Quarterly* and the *History of Higher Education Annual* are easily accessible and typically offer fascinating glimpses into the area.

An excellent guide to many of the current topical areas in the history of education is *Historical Inquiry in Education: A Research Agenda* (Best, 1983). This short and very readable book is comprised of essays describing 15 different methods of historical inquiry in education. The list includes institutional, biographic, quantitative, oral, intellectual, curricular and policy analysis, comparative and cross cultural history of education, regional studies, ethnic and minority study, urban communities, the history of women, the history of childhood, and the family and social history. For specifics, Shafer's *A Guide to the Historical Method* (1980) and Barzun and Graff's *The Modern Researcher* (1962) are both excellent sources of information and inspiration.

One of the most prolific authors in education is the U.S. Government. Often, government records are a rich source of data, especially for a quantitative history (Angus, 1983). State and local government documents can be equally lucrative in terms of historical interpretation and analysis.

Authors in the history of higher education vary dramatically in terms of focus, style, and quality of research. There are several books that deserve mention and can provide a basis for the reader interested in historical research and writing. In general, Brubacher and Rudy's *Higher Education in Transition: A History of American Colleges and Universities From 1636 to 1976* (3rd ed., 1976) is easy to read and varied in focus. Lawrence Veysey's *The Emergence of the American University* (1965) is an impressive and fascinating depiction of the modern, 20th century multiversity and the people who created it. Rudolph's *The American College and University* (1962) is a good overview as is Veblen's *The Higher Learning in America* (1957). For a different perspective, Bledstein offers his *The Culture of Professionalism: The Middle Class and the Development of Higher Education in America* (1978). Although this is by no means an inclusive listing, it should be enough to generate a list of other possibilities and connected works.

In the area of student life and research, the range of possibilities is quite extensive. Helen Horowitz's *Campus Life: Undergraduate Cultures from the 19th Century to the Present* (1987) is a good overview. More narrowly, Paula Fass concentrates on the student of the 1920s in *The Damned and the Beautiful: American Youth in the 1920s* (1977). Individual essays such as Patricia Graham's "Expansion and Exclusion: A History of Women in American Higher Education" (1978) can be most informative. Collected articles on college students such as Kuh, Bean, Hossler, and Stage's *ASHE Reader on the College Student* (1989) can be most helpful as well.

REFERENCES

Angus, D. L. (1983). The empirical mode: Quantitative history. In J. H. Best (Ed.), *Historical inquiry in education: A research agenda* (pp. 75–93). Washington, DC: American Educational Research Association.

Antler, J. (1987). *Lucy Sprague Mitchell.* New Haven, CT: Yale University Press.

Barzun, J., & Graff, H. F. (1962). *The modern researcher.* New York: Harcourt, Brace & World.

Belenky, M. F., Clinchy, B. M., Goldberger, N. R., & Tarule, J. M. (1986). *Women's ways of knowing: The development of self, voice, and mind.* New York: Basic Books.

Best, J. H. (Ed.). (1983). *Historical inquiry in education: A research agenda.* Washington, DC: American Educational Research Association.

Bledstein, B. J. (1978). *The culture of professionalism: The middle-class and the development of higher education in America.* New York: W. W. Norton.

Brubacher, J. S., & Rudy, W. (1976). *Higher education in transition: A history of American colleges and universities, 1636 to 1976* (3rd ed.). New York: Harper & Row.

Clark, T. A. (1914). College discipline. In M. A. Fulton (Ed.), *College life: Its condition and problems* (pp. 374–381). New York: Macmillan.

DiMartini, J. R. (1974). Student culture as a change agent in American higher education: An example from the 19th century. *Journal of Social History, 9,* 526–541.

Fass, P. (1977). *The damned and the beautiful: American youth in the 1920s.* New York: Oxford University Press.

Finnegan, T. (1990). Promoting "responsible freedom": Administrators and social fraternities at the University of Illinois, 1900–1931. *History of Higher Education Annual, 9,* 33–60.

Gilligan, C. (1982). *In a different voice: Psychological theory and women's development.* Cambridge, MA: Harvard University Press.

Graham, P. A. (1978). Expansion and exclusion: A history of women in American higher education. *Signs: Journal of Women in Culture and Society, 3,* 759–773.

Harlan, L. H. (1972). *Booker T. Washington: The making of a Black leader, 1856–1901.* Oxford: Oxford University Press.

Hodgkinson, H. L. (1985). *All one system: The demographics of American education.* Washington, DC: Institute for Educational Leadership.

Horowitz, H. L. (1986). *Alma mater: Design and experience in the women's colleges from their 19th century beginnings to the 1930s.* Boston: Beacon Press.

Horowitz, H. L. (1987). *Campus life: Undergraduate cultures from the end of the 19th century to the present.* Chicago: University of Chicago Press.

Jones, J. (1985). *Labor of love, labor of sorrow: Black women, work, and the family from slavery to the present.* New York: Basic Books.

Kaestle, C. F. (1988). Recent methodological developments in the history of American education. In R. M. Jaeger (Ed.), *Complementary methods for research in education* (pp. 61–80). Washington, DC: American Educational Research Association.

Kuh, G. K., Bean, J. P., Hossler, D., & Stage, F. K. (Eds.). (1989). *ASHE reader on college students.* Needham Heights, MA: Ginn Press.

Kliebard, H. M., & Franklin, B. M. (1983). The course of the course of study. In J. H. Best (Ed.), *Historical inquiry in education: A research agenda* (pp. 138–157). Washington, DC: American Educational Research Association.

Neustadt, R. E., & May, E. R. (1986). *Thinking in time: The uses of history for decision-makers.* New York: Free Press.

Rhatigan, J. J. (1978). A corrective look back. In J. R. Appleton, C. M. Briggs, & J. J. Rhatigan (Eds.), *Pieces of eight: The rites, roles, and styles of the dean by eight who have been there* (pp. 9–41). Portland, OR: NASPA Institute of Research and Development.

Robertson, J. O. (1980). *American myth, American reality.* New York: Hill and Wang.

Rudolph, F. (1962). *The American college and university.* New York: Knopf.

Saveth, E. N. (1988). The education of an elite. *History of Education Quarterly, 28,* 367–386.

Schmotter, J. W. (1990). "The best emissaries": MBA students at Cornell University, 1948–1987. *History of Higher Education Annual, 9,* 61–86.

Schwartz, R. A. (1990). *The feminization of a profession: Student affairs work in American higher education, 1890–1945.* Unpublished doctoral dissertation, Indiana University, Bloomington.

Shafer, R. J. (1980). *A guide to the historical method* (3rd ed.). Chicago: Dorsey.

Sherman, R. R., & Kirshner, J. (1976). *Understanding history of education.* Cambridge, MA: Schenkman.

Shulman, L. S. (1988). Disciplined inquiry in education: An overview. In R. M. Jaeger (Ed.), *Complementary methods for research in education* (pp. 3–23). Washington, DC: American Educational Research Association.

Solomon, B. M. (1985). *In the company of educated women: A history of women and higher education in America.* New Haven, CT: Yale University Press.

Thelin, J. R. (1982). *Higher education and its useful past: Applied history in research and planning.* Cambridge, MA: Schenkman.

Veblen, T. (1957). *The higher learning in America: A memorandum on the conduct of universities by business men.* New York: Sagamore Press.

Veysey, L. (1965). *The emergence of the American university.* Chicago: University of Chicago Press.

Warren, D. (1983). The federal interest: Politics and policy study. In J. H. Best (Ed.), *Historical inquiry in education: A research agenda* (pp. 158–179). Washington, DC: American Educational Research Association.

chapter 6

Document Analysis

Elizabeth J. Whitt

The palest ink is clearer than the best memory. (Chinese proverb in Holsti, 1969, p. 16)

Of the many potential sources of data about college students, one of the least used is documents (Lincoln & Guba, 1985). Documents tend to be ignored in favor of more active or interactive forms of qualitative (or verbal) data collection, such as interviews and observations. Nevertheless, documents are a useful and "ready-made source of data, easily accessible to the imaginative and resourceful investigator" (Merriam, 1988, p. 104). Consider the following items found at virtually every college or university: catalogues and student handbooks, long-range plans, mission statements, college histories, admissions viewbooks, minutes from student government meetings, advancement videos, posters advertising student activities, dining hall table tents, and letters from students to parents and friends. All can be considered documents for the purposes of discovering and understanding the nature of student life.

This chapter begins with a description of types of documents relevant to the study of college and university student experiences and ways in which such documents can be (and have been) used in research in higher education and student affairs. Means of collecting data from documents are then explored, and techniques for document analysis are presented. The chapter concludes with a discussion of the advantages and limitations of using documents as data sources.

79

TYPES AND USES OF DOCUMENTS

Definition of Documents

In 1969, Holsti defined a document as any written communication, but technological developments in the last two decades have resulted in an expanded definition: Lincoln and Guba (1985) defined a document as "any written or recorded material" (p. 27) not prepared for the purposes of the research or at the request of the inquirer. Merriam (1988) defined documents as materials available prior to the research, including written records or communications, physical evidence (of use, traffic, and so forth), and audio and video recordings.

Types of Documents

Documents can be divided into two major categories: public records and personal documents (Guba & Lincoln, 1981; Whitt, in press). Public records are materials created and kept for the purpose of "attesting to an event or providing an accounting" (Lincoln & Guba, 1985, p. 277). Public records that may be useful for research about college student experiences include student transcripts and records, institutional mission statements, annual reports, budgets, grade reports, meeting minutes, internal memoranda, research reports, policy manuals, institutional histories, faculty and student handbooks, official correspondence (Fetterman, 1989), demographic material (Goetz & LeCompte, 1984), mass media reports and presentations (Merriam, 1988), and descriptions of program development and evaluation (Patton, 1990).

Personal documents are first-person accounts of events and experiences (Merriam, 1988). Plummer (1983) stated that:

> the world is crammed full of personal documents. . . . People keep diaries, send letters, take photos, write memos . . . scrawl graffiti, publish their memoirs, write letters to the paper, leave suicide notes . . . shoot film, paint pictures . . . and try to record their personal dreams. (p. 13)

These "documents of life" (p. 13) include other items that may be useful for studying college students: calendars, schedules, scrapbooks, advertisements, banners, bulletin boards, buttons, and T shirts.

Uses of Documents

Documents, like other sources of qualitative data, enable the researcher to discover information, insights, and meanings relevant to his or her research purposes (Merriam, 1988; Whitt & Kuh, 1991). Unlike other sources of qualitative data, such as interviews and observations, documents are "unobtrusive" (Fetterman, 1989, p. 68); collecting data from documents is relatively invisible to, and requires minimal cooperation from, persons within the setting being studied, a point to which I shall return later.

Documents typically have been used by researchers in two ways. First, documents are primary data sources that provide direct information about events, decisions, activities, and processes (Patton, 1990). For example, student handbooks usually delineate, among other things, expectations for student behavior and opportunities for student involvement in out-of-class activities. College catalogues set forth the institution's mission and describe academic policies, programs, and staff. These data can provide insights into institutional processes, values, and participants (Goetz & LeCompte, 1984).

Information from documents also can be used to generate interview questions or identify events to be observed; in this sense, documents are secondary data sources (Whitt, in press; Whitt & Kuh, 1991). Admissions materials may, for example, raise questions about the clarity of the institution's mission in the minds of prospective students and their parents—questions that can be pursued in interviews with students and administrators. Institutional histories often identify traditions that the researcher ought to observe firsthand in order to understand campus life. Documents, interviews, and observations should be used to supplement, complement, and reinforce one another in order to obtain as complete a picture of the setting or phenomena being studied as is possible (Patton, 1990).

Public Records

Public records are particularly useful in describing institutional characteristics, such as backgrounds and academic performance of students, and in identifying institutional strengths and weaknesses, such as human and financial resources or consistency in what the organization says about itself to internal and external audiences; institutional values, such as commitment to diversity or the importance of out-of-class experiences for achieving the institution's mission; processes, such as resource allocation, hiring, and evaluation; priorities and concerns, such as physical plant improvements or student discipline; and official positions, such as admissions and hiring criteria and long-range plans (Fetterman, 1989).

Personal Documents

Personal documents can help the researcher to understand how the creator/author/writer sees her or his world and what she or he wants to communicate to an audience. A letter from students to their best friends, if available to the researcher, may provide rich information about how they perceive their experiences at the college and how they feel those experiences have affected them.

Documents of life (Plummer, 1983) also provide information about the context in which they are created. For example, what messages might be conveyed by empty public area bulletin boards and the absence of posters advertising student events on a campus? What might be inferred from a plethora of campaign posters promoting candidates for student government elections? (Any such messages obtained should, however, be explored by talking with people on the campus.) Thus, personal documents can reveal individual, inner experience while adding to the total picture of college student experiences at a particular institution (Merriam, 1988; Plummer, 1983).

An Example From Student Affairs Research

One example of the use of documents in examining and understanding college student experiences can be found in the College Experiences Study, a study of high-quality out-of-class experiences for undergraduates at 14 colleges and universities (Kuh et al., 1991). In that study, documents served as a means to learn about the institutional context and as a secondary data source, in that they provided topics and questions for interviews (Whitt & Kuh, 1991).

Documents, all of which could be considered public records, were obtained in advance of the visits to the campuses. Documents that were found to be particularly helpful in understanding student experiences included handbooks for faculty, students, and staff that contained policies and procedures; promotional pamphlets, such as admissions viewbooks and student organization recruitment brochures; institutional mission and goal statements; student newspapers; institutional histories; and other documents that referred to the integration of students' out-of-class experiences with the academic mission of the institution.

Other relevant documents came to our attention during campus visits. These included video tapes and slide presentations used for institutional advancement and recruitment purposes, planning documents, and table tents advertising student events and activities in the dining halls. We also gathered many useful impressions and questions by studying the documents of life that could be found in the environment: posters, bulletin boards, kiosks, banners, the messages on students' clothing, and so forth. We noted, for example, that we saw almost no Wichita State University (WSU) students wearing WSU T shirts, jackets, or hats. Could that be construed to indicate a lack of identification with the university? A lack of school spirit? A lack of funds to buy such items? A reluctance on the part of adult learners (the majority of WSU students) to take on the trappings of traditional student life? When we asked students about this, they said that no one wore such clothes on campus because "we all have jobs, and you can't wear those clothes to work." They also told us that if we had looked more closely, we would have seen WSU key chains, WSU license plate holders, and WSU notebooks— ways to express school identification and spirit that fit the nontraditional lifestyles of WSU students (Andreas, Kuh, Lyons, & Whitt, 1989).

The WSU experience was an effective reminder not to jump to conclusions about the meaning of data being collected. In the following section, methods of collecting and analyzing data from documents are explored.

TECHNIQUES FOR DATA COLLECTION AND ANALYSIS

When using qualitative research methods, the processes of data collection and analysis are conducted concurrently. By conducting data collection and analysis simultaneously, the results of analysis can be used to adjust data collection strategies in order to achieve greater understanding (e.g., conduct more observations and fewer interviews) (Marshall & Rossman, 1989) and provide a focus for data collection so that needless repetition and overwhelming quantities of data are minimized (Merriam, 1988). Collecting and analyzing data at the same time also allow the researcher to fill gaps in knowledge and understanding as they appear (Lincoln & Guba, 1985). This section begins with a brief discussion of ways to evaluate the usefulness of a particular document as a potential data source. Then procedures for collecting data are described, and one technique for analyzing documentary data is briefly explained.

Appropriateness and Credibility of the Document

Before beginning the process of collecting data from documents, the researcher must first ascertain the usefulness of the document as a data source (Merriam, 1988). "One needs a clear awareness of the document's significance: what it tells us about the site that's important" (Miles & Huberman, 1984, p. 51). That is, does the document provide insights or information that are relevant to the purposes of the research (Merriam, 1988)? A residence hall handbook, for example, although easily obtained, may or may not be an appropriate data source in a study of the experiences of adult learners. An institutional advancement video may provide important information about the image a college portrays to external audiences but might or might not be relevant to understanding student cultures. The questions that guide the research will determine whether a document is useful or not.

Criteria for ensuring and asserting the trustworthiness and credibility of qualitative research have been discussed in detail in a number of other works, including Fetterman (1989), Lincoln and Guba (1985), Marshall and Rossman (1989), Merriam (1988), and Patton (1990) as well as in this publication (in chapter 4). Establishing the credibility of documents—"How does one know that the document is what it purports to be?" (Guba & Lincoln, 1981, p. 238)—poses special problems for researchers. For example,

> [d]ocuments . . . , especially formal documents, sometimes have a semi-hypnotic effect on the minds of those who use them, and it is important to remember that all documents have been produced by fallible and potentially dishonest human beings, and that before they reach the scholar they may have passed through the hands of others who may also have had their failings. (Clark, cited in Guba & Lincoln, 1981, p. 239)

Therefore, the researcher must take care to assess the credibility of the document and, when in doubt, use other documents or other sources of data regarding the event or phenomenon at issue.

Guba and Lincoln (1981) offered a series of questions that should be addressed to a document to determine its credibility, including:

- What is the history of the document and how did it come into my possession?
- What guarantee is there that it is what it purports to be?
- Is the document complete and as it was originally created, or has it been tampered with or edited in any way?
- Who was the author, and is there any way to know whether he or she was likely to tell the truth about this particular event or matter?
- What were the author's sources of information and what were his or her purposes in developing it?
- Are the author's biases evident? If so, what are they, and how do they affect the credibility of the document?
- Are there other documents that could shed additional light on the information contained in this document, and how might those documents be obtained?

Data Collection

Once a document is obtained and determined to be an appropriate data source, data must be collected from the document. Merriam (1988) compared collecting data from documents and from interviews and observations in the following way:

Although the search [in both] is systematic, both settings also allow for the accidental uncovering of valuable data. Tracking down leads, being open to new insights, and being sensitive to the data are the same whether one is interviewing, observing, or analyzing documents. Since the investigator is the prime instrument for gathering data, he or she relies on skills and intuition to find and interpret data from documents. (p. 115)

Thus, the process of collecting data from documents is both systematic, in that it is purposeful and aims for accuracy, and flexible, in that the possibility of finding unexpected insights and information is appreciated. A *systematic* data collection process can be facilitated by the use of document summary forms (Miles & Huberman, 1984). These forms help to ensure that the same kind of information, such as content summaries and major themes inferred from the contents, is obtained from all documents, and help the researcher keep track of questions generated for use in interviews (Whitt & Kuh, 1991). A *flexible* data collection process depends on the researcher's ability to keep an open mind and acknowledge that she or he is probably not aware of all that must be known about the setting or all of what can be learned from the documents that have been obtained. The researcher must, for example, be willing to assume that there are documents that might be useful that she or he has yet to learn about, and that some documents believed at first to be important are not.

The process of collecting data from documents is similar to an interview, but in this case, the interviewee is the document. Questions that should be posed to the document include (Fetterman, 1989; Goetz & LeCompte, 1984; Whitt & Kuh, 1991):

- What is the title of the document?
- For what purposes and by whom was it produced?
- By whom and for what purposes might it be used?
- What information does the document contain?
- What themes or patterns (relevant to the research questions) can be gleaned from that information?
- What is the significance of the document for the study?
- What further questions does the document generate?
- In what ways is the document consistent or inconsistent with other sources of information about the setting?

Qualitative Content Analysis

Qualitative data analysis is inductive, using small units of data to develop larger categories, patterns, and themes, and, hence, interpretations and findings (Lincoln & Guba, 1985). Procedures typically used in inductive analysis of qualitative data include organization of data, generation of categories and themes, testing of emerging hypotheses against the data, seeking alternative explanations for data by challenging the themes that seem to be emerging, and writing a report of the findings (Marshall & Rossman, 1989). Several techniques have been developed to organize and analyze data collected from documents, including *qualitative content analysis.*

Content analysis of documents is concerned with systematic description of the content of communication (e.g., answering questions of What?, How? and To Whom?) (Guba & Lincoln, 1981; Holsti, 1969; Merriam, 1988). Content analysis is also used to make inferences about the causes and effects of the content (Holsti, 1969). For example, what might be the impact of alcohol policies on students' behavior? In what ways do statements in the institutional mission about the importance of student involvement in learning influence students' out-of-class activities?

The technique of qualitative content analysis (sometimes referred to as ethnographic content analysis) was developed from traditional, or quantitative, content analysis (Altheide, 1987). The differences, however, are that the data in qualitative content analysis are words (rather than numbers); data analysis is directed toward finding and understanding meanings and insights (rather than measuring frequency and verifying hypotheses); data collection and analysis are conducted by means of interaction between researcher and document (rather than by means of structured protocol and statistical procedures); and the product of the analysis is conveyed in words (rather than tables) (Altheide, 1987).

The process of qualitative content analysis involves developing rules for the analysis process (e.g., what content will be analyzed and what will not, how content will be selected for analysis); coding data (i.e., identifying units of data, such as words, phrases, or sentences and constructing categories from the units), interpreting the data (i.e., identifying themes or patterns in the categories), and drawing conclusions about the meaning of the themes or patterns (Guba & Lincoln, 1981; Holsti, 1969; Lincoln & Guba, 1985; Merriam, 1988). The document summary forms referred to earlier in this chapter can serve as a basis for identifying categories and themes across documents and/or across documents collected by multiple researchers (e.g., Whitt & Kuh, 1991).

A number of authors offer more thorough descriptions of the content analysis process than is possible in this chapter (e.g., Guba & Lincoln, 1981; Holsti, 1969). What should be noted here is that qualitative content analysis is an iterative process of constructing categories from the data and testing those categories against the data as well as "drawing of inferences on the basis of appearance or nonappearance of attributes in messages . . ." (Holsti, 1969, p. 10).

ADVANTAGES AND DISADVANTAGES OF USING DOCUMENTS AS DATA SOURCES

Documents have both strengths and limitations as sources of data in research regarding college student experiences. Researchers ought to understand these limitations so that information obtained from documents can be supplemented with data from other sources. In this section, the advantages and disadvantages are described and methods to cope with the disadvantages are offered.

Advantages of Documents

Documents offer a variety of advantages to the researcher. First, and maybe foremost, they are readily available (Lincoln & Guba, 1985)—in many cases more available than people to interview or events to observe. Many documents that will be useful in a study of student experiences are a matter of public record and/or are routinely sent upon request, such as admissions materials or catalogues. These documents can provide useful information about a college or university that serves as a basis for interviews and observations. Documents also are usually available at little or no cost, except, perhaps, for postage and/or copying (Merriam, 1988).

Second, documents are a stable source of data. That is, the researcher can collect, and analyze, data from them without altering them (Lincoln & Guba, 1985). Collecting data from documents is unlike more obtrusive forms of data collection that require interactions with respondents, such as interviews or observations. The presence of the interviewer/observer and the process of the interview/observation are likely to influence, in some way, the behavior or perceptions of the person being interviewed or observed. Thus, documents can be considered to be "more objective sources of data when compared to other forms" (Merriam, 1988, p. 108–109).

Third, documents are grounded in the setting and the language in which they occur and so "[help] the inquirer to maintain interest in the context and [help] to ensure that research is not removed from its social, historical, or political frame of reference" (Guba & Lincoln, 1981, p. 234). The context in which each college or university exists, including its history, geography, student body, and so forth, are reflected in its documents; its planning documents, viewbooks, missions statements, and handbooks are, in some ways, unique, and understanding that uniqueness is an important aspect of understanding the nature of student experiences at that institution. (Chapter 5 provides additional insights into the use of institutional documents in historical research.)

Finally, the use of documents may be the *only* way to study some aspects of a setting or phenomenon, such as issues that may not be observable or that are difficult to discuss (Merriam, 1988; Patton, 1990). Student records may, for example, be the best way to get specific information about incoming characteristics of students. Firsthand accounts of historical events and traditions may be available only in campus histories. There also may be issues about which the researcher could not know to ask without the use of documents (Patton, 1990). For example, although a college's mission statement emphasizes student responsibility and initiative, the student handbook is full of rules and regulations and policies that imply students' lives are very much a matter of institutional control; this apparent discrepancy can be explored in interviews with students, faculty, and administrators.

Disadvantages of Documents

Documents do, however, have limitations as data sources. First, they may be incomplete. Documents might not be sufficiently focused on the purposes of the research (because they were not, of course, developed for those purposes), or they might provide insufficient detail (Merriam, 1988; Patton, 1990). Planning documents, for example, focus on where the college wants to be in a certain period of time and so can provide more information about what the college desires to become than what it is. Student newspapers may refer to events or incidents that have already occurred and about which the researcher is unaware. Also, because documents present the perspectives or purposes of the persons who produced them, they may reflect only the position or negative aspects of an issue (Patton, 1990). Documents developed by an admissions office typically emphasize the strengths of the college and so can provide only one part of the picture of student experiences.

Second, documents may be inaccurate or of questionable authenticity, a problem that was described in the discussion on credibility (Merriam, 1988; Patton, 1990). Recall that the matter of determining accuracy and authenticity of documents should be expected to be part of the research process.

Finally, the unreactive nature of documents (that gives them their stability as data sources) can also be a disadvantage. Documents raise questions that they cannot answer, and there are limits to the amount of probing a researcher can do. Once the document has given all it can, there is no more. The researcher must be prepared, then, to use interviews and observations to answer questions generated by documents and to supplement or reinforce the information obtained in documents (Patton, 1990).

In general, the advantages of using documents as data sources outweigh the disadvantages in that the disadvantages can be minimized by other means of data collection and other sources of data. The availability, accessibility, stability, and potential richness of documents make them an important data source.

CONCLUSION

Effective use of documents should be part of the skills a student affairs researcher brings to her or his work (Patton, 1990). Although they may not provide the challenges or excitement of interviewing or observing, documents are a potentially fruitful source of both primary and secondary data and, as such, demand attention in any study of college student experiences. Bear in mind the words of Guba and Lincoln (1981):

> The guiding rule for choice of methods is which of the techniques available provides more data, better data, and data at lower cost than other methods. Further, a source that is replete with clues as to the nature of the context should never be ignored, whatever other inquiry methods one chooses. (p. 236)

FURTHER READING

A number of useful discussions of documents as data sources are available. Interested readers and researchers are referred to *Ethnography: Step by Step,* by David Fetterman (1989); *Naturalistic Inquiry,* by Yvonna Lincoln and Egon Guba (1985); *Case Study Research in Education: A Qualitative Approach,* by Sharan Merriam (1988); and *Qualitative Evaluation and Research Methods* (2nd ed.), by Michael Quinn Patton (1990). All of these texts (for complete publication data see the following reference list) provide clear and helpful descriptions of qualitative research methods.

REFERENCES

Altheide, D. L. (1987). Ethnographic content analysis. *Qualitative sociology,* *10*(1), 65–77.

Andreas, R., Kuh, G. D., Lyons, J. W., & Whitt, E. J. (1989). *Final report: Wichita State University.* Bloomington, IN: College Experiences Study.

Fetterman, D. M. (1989). *Ethnography: Step by step* (Applied Social Research Methods Series, Vol. 17). Newbury Park, CA: Sage.

Goetz, J. P., & LeCompte, M. D. (1984). *Ethnography and qualitative design in educational research.* Orlando, FL: Academic Press.

Guba, E. G., & Lincoln, Y. S. (1981). *Effective evaluation.* San Francisco: Jossey-Bass.

Holsti, O. (1969). *Content analysis for the social sciences and humanities.* Reading, MA: Addison-Wesley.

Kuh, G. D., Schuh, J. H., Whitt, E. J., Andreas, R., Lyons, J., Strange, C. C., Krehbiel, L., & MacKay, K. (1991). *Involving colleges: Successful approaches to encouraging student learning and personal development.* San Francisco: Jossey-Bass.

Lincoln, Y. S., & Guba, E. G. (1985). *Naturalistic inquiry.* Beverly Hills, CA: Sage.

Marshall, C., & Rossman, G. B. (1989). *Designing qualitative research.* Newbury Park, CA: Sage.

Merriam, S. B. (1988). *Case study research in education: A qualitative approach.* San Francisco: Jossey-Bass.

Miles, M. B., & Huberman, A. M. (1984). *Qualitative data analysis: A sourcebook of new methods.* Beverly Hills, CA: Sage.

Patton, M. Q. (1990). *Qualitative evaluation and research methods* (2nd ed). Newbury Park, CA: Sage.

Plummer, K. (1983). *Documents of life.* London: Allen & Unwin.

Whitt, E. J. (in press). Artful science: A primer on qualitative research methods. *Journal of College Student Development.*

Whitt, E. J., & Kuh, G. D. (1991). The use of qualitative methods in a team approach to multiple institution studies. *Review of Higher Education, 14*(3), 317–337.

chapter 7

The Ethnographic Interview

Kathleen Manning

The interview is a central data collection technique in qualitative research. The importance of the interview depends on the focus of the study (see the discussion in chapter 4 for information on the focus of a case study) and the kind of research being pursued. The interview may not be as prominent in historical research, which requires document analysis, but might be used in oral history research or an interview with a historical figure. Similarly, a study requiring extensive observation (e.g., studying college ceremonies) also will be less dependent on interviewing than on observing events, meetings, and activities. Ethnographic interviewing is used primarily when the researcher is seeking to discover the meaning that people construct from their involvement in a community (e.g., member of fraternity) or particular activity (e.g., orientation).

As with any technique, there are advantages and disadvantages when conducting ethnographic interviews. The advantages of interviewing include the face-to-face contact with respondents, opportunity for the researcher to explore topics in depth, ability to experience the affective as well as cognitive aspects of the respondents' responses, and depth of understanding gained. Disadvantages of interviewing include its labor-intensive and time-consuming nature, volume of information produced, difficulty of translating the information into field notes, and commitment necessary on the part of respondents.

This chapter describes techniques for using the ethnographic interview as a means to collect data in a qualitative research study. The topics in the chapter include the steps of the ethnographic interview: gaining access, choosing respondents, contacting respondents, preparing for the interview, conducting the interview, postinterview procedures, and performing data analysis.

GAINING ACCESS

The first step in the ethnographic interview process is to gain access to the research site and people within that community. Qualitative research is conducted in the field and, therefore, requires a gatekeeper to assist the researcher in gaining access to the community. The tasks of the gatekeeper include identifying potential respondents, introducing the researcher to the community, and serving as a key respondent. An essential role of the gatekeeper is to provide the researcher with verbal introductions to the community. For example, if as part of a campus-wide assessment on the quality of life, a student affairs division is conducting a study of a substance-free residence hall, the researcher may use the dean of students and/or the residence director of the hall as gatekeepers through which to gain access to students and other respondents. Potential respondents could be identified from students and staff members associated with the hall and recommended to the researcher. As involved partners in the research process, the dean of students and residence director talk about the study as part of their daily routines. This way the community knows that the research is occurring.

The gatekeeper also may be a respondent, but this is not a necessity. Choosing respondents should be a carefully considered methodological decision as the researcher may have compelling reasons to keep the gatekeeper and respondent functions separate. For example, if the gatekeeper is a close friend, that person may be an unsatisfactory choice as a respondent.

The gatekeeper should be someone with whom the researcher can establish excellent rapport. This is most often a relationship that lasts for the duration of the research. He or she may be called upon for a variety of purposes throughout the data collection: reading the complete set of field notes (also known as grand member checking), providing advice about the viability of the emerging interpretations, and serving as a source of moral support. The gatekeeper-researcher relationship should be such that the researcher can seek this person out for advice and guidance. If the gatekeeper is involved in the study, he or she can be a peer debriefer (i.e., someone who is knowledgeable about the study with whom the researcher can discuss the study's progress and frustrations) as well as a confidant and colleague. In an ongoing fashion an involved gatekeeper could be cognizant of people who could serve as interesting respondents and might be willing to identify additional respondents after the initial contacts have been identified and interviewed.

CHOOSING RESPONDENTS

The second step of the ethnographic interview process is choosing the types of respondents to be sought for the study. This step is a major task of the research. The goal is to locate and make contact with people who are well informed about the topic being researched and willing to share that information with the researcher.

Patton (1980) suggested a technique called *purposive* or *theoretical sampling*. Through this technique, the research topic can be explored in depth through the identification of a wide range of respondents. The strategies for obtaining this wide range and depth of information through respondent choice include purposively sampling (Lincoln, 1985) for the following: (a) extreme or deviant cases, (b) typical cases, (c) maximum variation cases, (d) critical cases, and (e) politically important or sensitive cases.

Sampling in this manner does not seek representativeness or randomness of a population as a goal. Due to the fact that generalization to the wider population is not a goal of this style of research, the researcher is seeking an informed point of view rather than representativeness for generalizing. The goals, then, are an informed approach to different perspectives on the topic, wide scope of opinion, and richness of information gained from people with a range of experiences and feelings about the topic.

In the substance-free residence hall example, respondents purposively or theoretically sampled could include the following: extreme or deviant cases (e.g., students who lived in the hall for a short period of time and moved out), typical cases (e.g., students who have chosen to live in the hall but do not hold leadership positions in the hall), maximum variation cases (e.g., students who have lived in the hall for the duration of their undergraduate years), critical cases (e.g., students who wanted to live in the hall but were denied access for some reason), and politically important or sensitive cases (e.g., resident assistants).

Qualitative researchers often are queried about the number of respondents necessary for a well-done study. Without representativeness as a goal, numbers recede from being a major issue with purposive sampling. Respondents should be chosen and interviewed until the researcher feels that (a) he or she is hearing redundant information, (b) the categories generated in analysis (see chapter 4) are saturated, and

(c) the multiple perspectives present in the community are well represented in the data collected.

CONTACTING RESPONDENTS

The third step in the ethnographic interview process is the time-consuming task of contacting respondents. This step can be a stressful and trying one for the novice researcher as respondents are asked to share their "meaning-making processes," feelings about a topic, and life experiences.

Interviews as guided conversations (Bogdan & Biklen, 1982; Lincoln & Guba, 1985) focused on meaning and feelings are educational and enlightening experiences for respondents. Because people generally enjoy talking about themselves, their experiences, and topics about which they are interested, respondents are often quite willing and anxious to talk to researchers. Respondents' willingness is often more evident than expected by the novice qualitative researcher. The real dilemmas and often-unanticipated setbacks with this step are logistical. These problems include time constraints on the respondent and researcher, delays when arranging schedules, and dilemmas locating respondents. These often require more time and patience to resolve than could ever be anticipated by the researcher. Although most often the researcher is a stranger to the community with few, if any, acquaintances, it is recommended that friends are not called upon to serve as respondents (Lincoln & Guba, 1985). The existence of dual relationships (e.g., friend and research participant) calls the ethics of the researcher into question.

Often it is helpful for the researcher to ask the gatekeeper to make the initial contact with a potential respondent. The gatekeeper is more familiar with the potential respondent and can explain the focus of the study and gauge his or her level of interest. This situation can save the researcher from making a "cold call" to a potential respondent who has no knowledge of the study and no acquaintance with the researcher. Unfortunately, a large study with multiple respondents might require a time commitment likely to be impossible for the gatekeeper to fulfill, but if the researcher has chosen his or her gatekeeper carefully as a person who is well respected in the community, the researcher can obtain permission to use the gatekeeper's name and status to gain access to respondents.

PREPARING FOR THE INTERVIEW

The fourth step in the ethnographic interview process is preparing for the interview. In order to gain the most information from the interview and maximize the comfort of the respondent, the researcher should consider all aspects of the interview as a means to gather data about the respondent and his or her culture. This can be partially achieved by asking the respondent his or her preference for interview location. The respondent can tell the researcher a great deal about the campus, assist in gaining access to locations difficult to venture into without a community member (e.g., residence halls), or to experience a place on campus about which the respondent was previously unaware. Possibilities for this level of data collection might include asking the respondent to meet the researcher in a place that is meaningful to him or her or to the topic being studied.

For example, in the substance-free study, it will be difficult for the researcher to walk in and observe the substance-free residence hall on a particular evening. If, however, the researcher is there on a respondent's invitation, then impressions formed about the hall can be added to the data gathered through the interview. This process saves time while deepening and expanding the impressions created through the interview.

An indispensable part of interview preparation is composing questions. More times than not these questions go unasked because the respondent eagerly talks about himself or herself. Ideally the interview should be left open-ended so that the respondent chooses the understandings and feelings to share. Questions prepared in advance cannot help but contain a priori assumptions the researcher has built into the questions. The researcher may choose to simply ask, "What do you think or feel about . . .?" "What would you like to tell me about . . .?" "What's going on here?" But question preparation is important because at times these questions are a necessary way to give the respondent a place to start and a way to understand the focus of the study. They also can be a means for the researcher to keep the conversation within the boundaries and focus of the study.

Questions written in advance serve as a way to train the researcher's thoughts about the research progress and interpretations emerging from the study. Question writing assists the researcher to keep his or her sights on the focus. They also serve as a way for the skilled qualitative researcher and interviewer to be prepared for all eventualities. It may be that the respondent expects the researcher to ask questions or has not thought about the focus. In the latter case, the respondent may *expect* to be guided or structured through the interview. When structuring the interview the qualitative researcher needs to set aside a priori assumptions and expectations about what will be found. The researcher should take care that these research questions do not become self-fulfilling prophesies. Questions written in advance of the interview contain the assumptions and a priori beliefs of the researcher. Even the most broadly written questions contain traces of the theories reviewed by the researcher and his or her expectations of what will be found through the research. The researcher must guard against the probability that "believing is seeing" rather than "seeing is believing" (Clark, 1985).

An important aspect of interview preparation is gathering information about the respondents' background culture. The researcher needs to go into the interview not with his or her mind made up but also not completely unaware of the respondent's background, culture, and education. The danger in being uninformed about the respondent is that inappropriate, uninformed, or, worse yet, insulting questions might be asked inadvertently.

The researcher also should be informed about the history and traditions of the community being studied. Conducting research in a community must include respect for the practices and common-sense knowledge of the community members. Ethical and respectful practice necessitates that researchers avail themselves of such information.

As community members, respondents have a great deal of tacit knowledge (Polanyi, 1983) about their community. Tacit knowledge is known but unexpressed by respondents. The interview often is the first time that the respondent discusses his or her meanings and understandings. Nonetheless, those understandings exist and are evident in behavior, actions, language, and ways of being in the community.

The researcher, at the start of the research, is the least informed person within the community being studied. This is particularly the case with qualitative research that aims to build theory grounded in the data collected within the research site. The respondents know more about the topic than the researcher possibly could. The short period of time that the researcher works in that community never can substitute for the experience of living in the community as a member. As an uninformed person within the community, the researcher must take care that he or she does not overly direct the interview. A respondent anxious to help the researcher may answer only the questions asked rather than venturing into community knowledge well known by the respondent but not obvious to the researcher. The goal is to leave the interview open-ended so the researcher collects information based on what the respondent feels is important rather than what the researcher feels is important.

The role of the researcher in preparing for the interview is to strike a balance between overstructuring the interview such that theory and a priori assumptions guide the research and understructuring the interview such that the interview is not focused and becomes useless as data collection. The preparation should not get in the way of hearing what the respondent is saying.

For example, a researcher conducting an assessment of the quality of campus life could broadly begin with the question "What do you feel about the quality of campus life?" After conversation about this question through the first or subsequent interviews, the data collected become more focused as the researcher becomes more knowledgeable. Categories are explored and gaps in the research are filled, and increasingly focused questions are composed and pursued. The questions at this time are more narrow in scope and intent.

CONDUCTING THE INTERVIEW

The fifth step of the ethnographic interview process is conducting the interview. Student affairs administrators are particularly suited to interviewing as they are well practiced in the arts of listening and attending, summarizing, and empathizing. These skills traditionally have been taught through student affairs preparation programs and utilized daily in administrative practice.

A helpful perspective for the researcher is one that considers the interview to be a gift the respondent has granted to the researcher. The interview is an investment as the respondent takes valuable time, effort, and, often, risk, to share his or her feelings, knowledge, and understandings. From this point of view, the interview is not an experience to be taken lightly. The researcher needs to be sure that he or she is prepared enough to communicate the value being placed on the interview as well as appreciation for the respondent's investment. To act in any less interested and respectful manner risks that the researcher may be perceived as ungracious toward the respondent's efforts.

Those in student affairs have a variety of data collection skills well suited for ethnographic interviewing. These skills include the listening and counseling skills of direct eye contact, minimal encouragers, attention to nonverbals, and listening for content and feelings (Egan, 1990). Data collection during an ethnographic interview is not completely unlike collecting information during an intake interview with a student, a disciplinary conference, or a job interview. The ethnographic interviewer, like the administrator exercising listening skills, listens for content as well as meaning and assumptions beneath and within the respondent's words. The ethnographic interview is less a process of recording the respondent's words than a process of attending to the meaning of those words, understanding and working through the respondent's beliefs and feelings.

The interviewer is advised that listening skills based on predominantly White perspectives may not be appropriate in interviews with people from nondominant cultural perspectives (e.g., African Americans, Latinos, Native Americans, women, international students). As examples, it would be inappropriate to expect direct eye contact with Native-American respondents (Locust, 1988), to sit too close to an Asian-American respondent (Atkinson, Morten, & Sue, 1989), or to misunderstand passionately expressed language used by African-American respondents (Kochman, 1981). The rule in these situations is to consider the comfort, needs, and style of the respondent in relation to the researcher's needs or goals of the study. Attention to the respondent's nonverbal cues about the appropriateness of physical proximity, eye contact, and other culture-specific aspects of interpersonal communication should be heeded. Preparing for an interview should include gathering information about the norms of the culture in which the researcher is studying.

A skillful interviewer often is needed to keep the respondent concentrated on the focus of the study. Without this effort to direct the interview toward the focus, the researcher may collect data that are interesting but unrelated to the study and its focus. In this case both the researcher and respondent's time is wasted as information that is interesting but of little use to the study is collected.

A significant aspect of the interview is to attend to the surroundings in an effort to understand the context in which the respondent constructs his or her meaning. What are the characteristics of the room? What do the surroundings say about the respondent? What is the context (e.g., institutional norms and assumptions, cultural practices, ways of operating) in which the respondent makes meaning? The interviewer may decide that the surroundings say nothing about the respondent or, conversely, that they say a great deal. The point is that the interviewer must attend to these details and circumstances in his or her effort to collect rich and meaningful data. Every aspect of the researcher or human as instrument is attuned to the context in which the data are shared. Data collection goes well beyond the respondent's words.

A primary aspect of the ethnographic interview is the trust and rapport necessary between the researcher and the respondent. Without such a relationship the researcher will be unable to develop an interview situation in which the respondent comfortably shares his or her feelings and understandings. This relationship generally requires two to three interviews to establish.

An aspect of qualitative research is the equal relationship of the respondent and researcher. The respondent is not a subject but a partner in the research process. As such, both researcher and respondent share the teacher and learner roles. Rather than a hierarchical relationship, it is more helpful to reduce the distance between the researcher and respondent so that both are equal partners in the research process (Freire, 1970; Lincoln & Guba, 1985).

During the interview, the researcher needs to record the data in such a way that he or she can retrieve the information for analysis at a later date. This recording process is determined by the researcher's personal style and system of organizing. There is no one correct way to record the data. Rather the interviewer must think through the data analysis process and base his or her recording techniques on that analysis. For example, will a tape recorder be used? Can the interviewer take cryptic notes that he or she later transcribes into an as complete as possible reconstruction of the entire interview? Will interpretations and observations be made during the interview or will the interviewer note the surroundings and write about them later?

Practices and suggestions that may assist the interviewer to plan data recording are as follows:

1. *Tell the respondent how you are planning to record the data during the interview (e.g., tape recorder, notes in a notebook).* Ethically, the question "Do you mind if I use a tape recorder?" must be asked of the respondent. The respondent also should be told in advance if the researcher will be taking notes during the interview. Otherwise, it may be disconcerting for the respondent to notice that his or her words are being noted without prior knowledge and preparation. The respondent should be given a choice about how his or her words are recorded. This is part of the comfort- and trust-building practices as well as the ethical practices of the research process.

2. *Always plan for the tape recorder to malfunction or fail to pick up the respondent's words.* Poor acoustics, dead batteries, and a host of other problems plague those who confidently rely on a tape recorder to carry out the majority of the data collecting. Furthermore, even when tape recorders are used, the interviewer should be writing reactions, interpretations, and impressions formed during the interview. To ignore this process puts the interviewer at risk of forgetting those impressions during the tape recording transcription. Lastly, transcription of the word-for-word interview recorded on tape often results in a tremendous volume of field notes. It might be fruitful to record the highlights and important aspects of the interview rather than to concentrate on capturing every word.

3. *Consider using a small notebook during the interview.* This notebook can be small enough to slip into a briefcase or purse. This allows notes to be recorded in a manner that enables the interviewer to

remain attentive to the respondent. For example, key words could be written down. These key words become a means to jog the interviewer's memory when he or she later reconstructs the entire interview as close to verbatim as possible. During this transcription questions for subsequent interviews become obvious and are recorded into the field notes. These questions are addressed in the next interview.

There is no way to predict during the interview or field note transcription the pieces of data that will emerge as a central theme, important consideration, or fundamental interpretation. Therefore, phrases may be written down from which a direct quote can be reconstructed. Words may be recorded to remember a situation or story to be reproduced from the interviewer's memory.

4. *Limit the interview to a certain amount of time (e.g., 1 hour), in consideration of the respondent's time.* This time limit should be discussed with the respondent during the first few minutes of the interview.

5. *Give the respondent a consent form to sign and discuss it during the first interview.* This form should outline the focus of the research, uses of the data and conclusions, and researcher's commitments. One of these commitments is that the respondent can choose to withdraw from the research at any time. He or she has a right to receive any field notes and/or recordings made that are based on his or her meanings, feelings, and understandings.

POSTINTERVIEW PROCEDURES

The sixth step of the interview process is the activities after the interview. At this time the field notes are given back to the respondents as part of the member-checking process.

These field notes with all their notations and interviewer comments are read (i.e., member checked) by the respondent. Member checking enables the respondent to check the field notes for faithfulness. In other words, do they convey the feelings, understandings, content, and meaning shared during the interview? These notes are edited by the respondent to clarify points missed by the researcher, add subsequent thoughts, and correct erroneous perceptions on the part of the respondent. The interpretations built through the research process also are checked by the respondent in a process of coconstruction. At each step in the process, the researcher remains acutely aware that he or she is the least knowledgeable person within the community. Respondents possess a well-formed understanding, particularly in the beginning stages of the research, of the college, its context, and the community's ways. For example, if a student affairs educator is conducting research on the quality of campus life, the students being interviewed are those with the most information about student opinion, feelings, and understandings. Unfortunately, student affairs educators often are placed in the precarious position of "experts" on student opinion. This expertise is put into practice during university policy and decision making. The expert role is one that student affairs educators *should* fulfill on campus, but this expertise must be grounded in research that is sound methodologically and ethically rather than built on opinion, educated guesses, or anecdotal impressions. This ethical practice includes research used on a local or campus level as well as that used on a national or profession level.

As part of the trust and rapport built during the interview process, the researcher, following the interview, will be well advised to send a hand-written thank you note together with the field notes for member checking and consent form.

There is no formula for the "correct" number of interviews to be held with a respondent. You should plan as many interviews as it takes for you to begin to hear redundant information. If the interviews remain centered on the focus of the study, there will come a point when the respondent has shared all or most of the information that he or she has on that subject. Any further interviewing is not likely to result in additional information.

During any additional interviewing, information and questions generated from the initial interviews should be folded back into the interview process. In this way, the interviews become more focused and, often, shorter in length.

PERFORMING DATA ANALYSIS

Chapter 4 goes into detail about analyzing data collected through interviewing. The process, unitizing and categorizing (Lincoln & Guba, 1985), involves transcribing and sorting heuristically sound bits of data in an effort to understand the themes emerging from the data.

Data analysis occurs throughout the interviewing process. In this way, holes in the data collection can be filled, emerging themes can be elaborated upon, and respondents can be involved in the generation of themes and interpretations that serve as the backbone for the final case study report.

Data are analyzed after each interview. The themes gleaned from the analysis are fed into the next interview in a process that builds upon itself. Data collection is concluded when the categories and themes generated through data analysis are saturated. The researcher knows that he or she is at this point when the information collected becomes redundant and repetitive.

CONCLUSION

The central issues in interviewing are the trust and rapport to be built with respondents. In this regard it is essential that the researcher remember that the respondent graciously is sharing information, knowledge, and understandings about his or her community. If this point of view or approach is maintained, many questions about ethical practice and appropriate behavior with respondents are raised and anticipated in advance of any discomfort on the part of the respondents.

As one of the most important tools of data collection, the interview should not be taken lightly. It is an experience for which the researcher should be prepared carefully. In particular, care should be taken so that the respondent has an opportunity to receive feedback about the research conclusions and interpretations. As community members who have a vested interest in what is written about their community, they have every right to be involved at each step of the research process. The interview should not be their only involvement in the research. Each respondent should be given the opportunity to learn something about him- or herself or the community through involvement in the research process.

In closing and in summary, the beginning qualitative researcher should remember that the interview is more similar to a dialogue and conversation than an inquisition. Its successful use depends on tact and consideration more than stellar technique. Finally, the growth experienced by the respondent is quite often matched by the growth of the researcher. When used carefully and skillfully, the interview is a time of learning for both the respondents and the researcher.

FURTHER READING

Agar, M. (1986). *Speaking of ethnography*. Beverly Hills, CA: Sage.
Eisner, E., & Peshkin, A. (1990). *Qualitative inquiry in education: The continuing debate*. New York: Teachers College Press.
Goetz, J., & LeCompte, M. (1984). *Ethnography and qualitative design in educational research*. New York: Academic Press.
Guba, E. (Ed.). (1990). *The paradigm dialog*. Beverly Hills, CA: Sage.

Kuhn, T. (1962). *The structure of scientific revolutions* (2nd ed.). Chicago: University of Chicago Press.

Lincoln, Y. (Ed.). (1985). *Organizational theory and inquiry: The paradigm revolution.* Beverly Hills, CA: Sage.

Spradley, J. (1979). *The ethnographic interview.* New York: Holt, Rinehart and Winston.

Taylor, S., & Bogdan, R. (1984). *Introduction to qualitative research methods: The search for meanings* (2nd ed.). New York: Wiley.

Van Maanen, J. (Ed.). (1979). *Qualitative methodology.* Beverly Hills, CA: Sage.

REFERENCES

Atkinson, D. R., Morten, G., & Sue, D. W. (Eds.). (1989). *Counseling American minorities: A cross cultural perspective* (3rd ed.). Dubuque, IA: William C. Brown.

Bogdan, R., & Biklen, S. (1982). *Qualitative research for education: An introduction to theory and methods.* Boston: Allyn and Bacon.

Clark, D. (1985). Emerging paradigms in organizational theory and research. In Y. Lincoln (Ed.), *Organizational theory and inquiry: The paradigm revolution* (pp. 43–78). Beverly Hills, CA: Sage.

Egan, G. (1990). *The skilled helper.* Pacific Grove, CA: Brooks/Cole.

Freire, P. (1970). *Pedagogy of the oppressed.* New York: Basic Books.

Kochman, T. (1981). *Black and White styles in conflict.* Chicago: University of Chicago Press.

Lincoln, Y. (1985). *Organizational theory and inquiry: The paradigm revolution.* Beverly Hills, CA: Sage.

Lincoln, Y., & Guba, E. (1985). *Naturalistic inquiry.* Beverly Hills, CA: Sage.

Locust, C. (1988). Wounding the spirit: Discrimination and traditional American-Indian belief systems. *Harvard Educational Review, 58,* 315–330.

Patton, M. (1980). *Qualitative research methods.* Beverly Hills, CA: Sage.

Polanyi, M. (1983). *The tacit dimension.* Gloucester, MA: Peter Smith.

chapter 8

Focus Groups: Teachable and Educational Moments for All Involved

Jill Ellen Carnaghi

Frequently student affairs work involves working with students in groups. Therefore, qualitative methods that involve groups to collect data may contribute significantly to an understanding of the topic under review and subsequent outcomes and information about the topic. The use of focus groups is one such qualitative tool that could have significant benefits for the inquirer, and one that is well worth exploring when conducting research or assessment activities within and among groups (Jacobi, 1991; Russell, 1991). The purpose of this chapter is to present the reader with information on focus groups, including a definition of focus groups, their relation to the concept of community, characteristics and use of focus groups, advantages and disadvantages, and steps in planning and conducting successful focus groups as well as in analyzing the data collected.

WHAT IS A FOCUS GROUP?

Krueger (1988) provided a concise definition of a focus group:

> . . . a carefully planned discussion designed to obtain perceptions on a defined area of interest in a permissive, nonthreatening environment.

> It is conducted with approximately 7 to 10 people by a skilled inter-
> viewer. The discussion is relaxed, comfortable, and often enjoyable for
> participants as they share their ideas and perceptions. Group members
> influence each other by responding to ideas and comments in the dis-
> cussion. (p. 18)

Morgan (1988) described a focus group as similar to group interviews;
however, the inquirer acts more as a facilitator than as an interviewer
to generate discussion *among* the members of the group. A focus group
is not a two-way exchange between the facilitator and individual focus
group members; a successful focus group involves discussion among
participants. Members usually do not know each other but do possess
some common characteristics related to the research topic (e.g., seniors
who use the placement office services, students returning to the residence halls for a second year, student leaders who live off campus,
returning women students who are single parents). Through the course
of the discussion, focus group members may change their opinions on
a topic many times over, and the focus group facilitator may ask for
clarification about these changing views. However, members are never
asked to reach consensus on a particular topic or to provide only one
answer or opinion to a posed question.

Initially, focus groups were used in the social sciences. As early as
1931, social scientists were expressing concern over the more traditional
ways of gathering data via a structured interview process in which the
interviewer takes the lead, has an established set of questions—often
closed-ended questions—and follows that prescribed list with no variation. Rice (1931) acknowledged the possibility that data collected via
structured interviewing may reflect the interviewer's biases and precon-
ceived opinions rather than the interviewee's views and beliefs. Non-
directive interviewing came into vogue in the 1930s and 1940s. More
recently, focus groups have been used extensively in marketing research,
and much of the literature written about focus groups has its origins in
the marketing realm (Advertising Research Foundation, 1985; Bartos,
1986; Bellenger, Bernhardt, & Goldstrucker, 1979). Within marketing
research, focus groups usually are used as a means to gauge the public's
interest in a particular product. Focus groups frequently are used to
react to television commercials, to access the effectiveness of advertising,
or to test potential products.

THE CONCEPT OF COMMUNITY AS IT RELATES
TO FOCUS GROUPS

Community as groups of individuals coming together for a shared purpose is a concept embedded in American life since its beginnings. In

the 1830s, Alex de Tocqueville studied American society and individuals' relationships and commitment to groups of people. As the Industrial Revolution took shape in this country, Americans became more dependent upon others for their basic needs. Work settings began to involve others from outside the extended family. Food could be purchased from others and did not always have to be raised in individual gardens. The moral development and spiritual lives of the children were no longer the sole responsibility of the woman in the family.

Bellah, Madsen, Sullivan, Swidler, and Tipton (1985) in *Habits of the Heart* wrote extensively about communities: communities of memory, the therapeutic quest for community, communities of interest, communities pertaining to church or civic affairs or politics, and so on. Because much of personal and professional lives involve working with, depending upon, sharing with, and learning from others, why shouldn't research methods also involve groups and obtaining valuable information from individuals within group settings?

The definition and some of the underlying assumptions of focus groups act in concert with many of the beliefs and activities of student affairs professionals, thereby making focus groups an excellent research tool for use by individuals within student affairs organizations. Many student affairs professionals apply the various elements that define *community* to their everyday work world, including shared values and common purpose, degree of social contact or proximity of students, commitment to working together, mutual dependence and sharing among members, time together, and agreed-upon group standards (Blimling & Miltenberger, 1984).

Student affairs staff purposefully and proactively work to have student groups develop and define a common purpose (e.g., behave responsibly with alcohol, help the homeless in the community), to promote interdependency to fulfill certain tasks and needs (e.g., conflict resolution, alcohol education), to define and live by mutually shared expectations for a group (e.g., quiet hours in a residence hall, prohibition of hazing activities in a sorority), and to respect and celebrate the unique differences among individual group members (e.g., slating club officers with diverse backgrounds, characteristics, and strengths).

Just as student affairs work involves people and groups of people interacting with one another, so do focus groups. Because focus groups are dependent upon group interaction and discussion to gain information on a particular issue, the focus group facilitator wants to generate as much discussion as possible among focus group members. As members listen to each other and express differing attitudes and opinions on a topic, opinions begin to shift and new opinions are formulated. The facilitator observes and probes further regarding areas of particular interest. "The intent of the focus group is to promote self-disclosure among participants" (Krueger, 1988, p. 23). The interactive, informal group environment facilitates discussion and gives even the most reserved or introverted individual the opportunity to talk in a relatively low-risk setting. "The hallmark of focus groups is *the explicit use of the group interaction to produce data and insights that would be less accessible without the interaction found in a group*" (Morgan 1988, p. 12). Student affairs work is teeming with groups that are attempting to form communities among themselves, and methodology used in conducting research or assessment within student affairs should take advantage of these many group settings.

CHARACTERISTICS OF FOCUS GROUPS

Krueger (1988) identified the following characteristics of focus groups: each consists of individuals who have specific characteristics and who provide information that is qualitative and collected through a directed discussion.

As stated earlier, focus groups usually consist of 7 to 10 people. In a specific instance, the inquirer may have justification for considering a group smaller than 7 or larger than 10. If the topic is of a very sensitive nature (e.g., needs of special student populations, obtaining information on how minority students have been treated on a predominantly White campus), the inquirer may want to create a more intimate and "safe" environment that may be easier to obtain with fewer individuals. However, the group should be large enough to ensure the exchange of opinions. If time is of the essence and the topic is not particularly sensitive, then it may be advantageous to conduct fewer groups with larger numbers of individuals per group. The facilitator must guard against multiple conversations occurring simultaneously within various subgroups.

In thinking about the ideal size of a focus group, it is also important to consider where the discussion will occur. A room large enough to accommodate all group members is needed, with seating so that all members are able to sit at the same level and establish eye contact with one another. The room should provide privacy and be free of interruptions as well as located in a building that is easy to find and where parking is not a problem.

Although the ideal focus group is made up of strangers, they should share some commonalities. In general, researchers should avoid selecting members having extreme differences in class (e.g., a first-time, first-year student and a senior), in age (e.g., a traditional age student and an older, returning woman student), or in living arrangements (e.g., a fraternity member and a commuter student). The sooner the group members recognize some commonalities among themselves and feel their opinions will not be "put down" by someone in a "higher position," the sooner they will begin to relax and talk more openly about their true feelings and opinions on the topic. Remember, homogeneity and commonality among members is the ideal when it comes to characteristics of group members; however, the inquirer is not looking for homogeneity and commonality of opinions and perspectives. Differences in points of view among members may lead to potentially more exciting and dynamic discussions. On occasion, members of a focus group may know each other (e.g., students who have taken classes together, student leaders who know many people on campus). In this instance, the importance of moving beyond previous, mutual experiences to independent, current thinking must be stressed.

A student affairs professional is likely to have been involved in or facilitated countless numbers of groups (e.g., committee work, group interviews to fill vacant positions, staff development and training workshops). However, the inquirer may want to stop and think twice before assigning herself or himself the role of focus group facilitator. If the researcher is in a position of power over focus group members (e.g., a dean of students talking with students about a proposed code of ethics and the discipline system, a resident director facilitating a group of resident adviser applicants to find out their perceptions of what type of learning occurs in a residence hall), the data most likely will be biased and not representative of members' true perceptions and opinions. The actual content of discussions is the data that are interesting and important to collect; the inquirer is not trying to quantify information as much as he or she is trying to identify recurring themes.

THE USE OF FOCUS GROUPS IN STUDENT AFFAIRS RESEARCH AND ASSESSMENT

Focus groups are gaining in popularity as inquirers are interested in gaining a more in-depth understanding of an organization's culture, environment, or the context surrounding particular problems. Focus groups can stand alone or be used in conjunction with other qualitative or quantitative research methods (Morgan, 1988; Krueger, 1988). Focus groups often are used in conducting exploratory or preliminary research or as follow-up to other research methods.

In this vein, focus groups are useful for:

- orienting oneself to a new field
- generating hypotheses based on informants' insights
- evaluating different sites or study populations
- developing interview schedules and questionnaires
- getting participants' interpretations of results from earlier studies. (Morgan, 1988, p. 11)

However, it is also important to consider the use of focus groups as a self-contained means of collecting data. In many areas involving student affairs work and the need to obtain information on individuals' experiences, attitudes, or perceptions, it may be perfectly legitimate to use focus groups as the sole means for data collection.

A new dean of students may use focus groups to discover students' perceptions of the campus environment and out-of-classroom learning experiences. A director of student activities may bring together groups of student leaders to help interpret the results of a student government survey pertaining to the use of activities fees. When renovating a student union is being considered, focus groups consisting of frequent users of the existing structure may be able to identify future uses of the facility; this information then can be shared with the architects.

Student affairs professionals can take some lessons from those involved in marketing as well as those in the nonprofit sector when it comes to using focus groups to their advantage. Student affairs work involves providing any number of services and programs primarily to students, but the "client" also could include students' parents, graduates, townspeople, or prospective students. Why not utilize focus groups prior to, during, or as a follow-up to a particular program (e.g., soliciting student input in developing an academic orientation for transfer students, collecting students' perceptions throughout the semester regarding the leadership class they are taking, asking for feedback on wellness programs sponsored by the student health center)? Focus groups can provide information when the student government is considering increasing activities fees, when the health center wants to learn why more women do not take advantage of the free gynecological exams it offers, or when next year's planning group for summer orientation wants feedback from current first-time, first-year students regarding their perceptions about this past summer's orientation.

Krueger (1988) identified the possible uses of focus groups prior to a program: collecting information for a survey, using information to do a needs assessment, conducting a "test-run" of a new program or idea, or probing students for what they consider when making decisions. During a program, focus groups can assist in attracting additional students to an already existing program that has low attendance or in evaluating programs currently in progress (e.g., soliciting impressions and reactions to the "Women on Wheels Program"—a women's transportation service intended to ensure women's safety at night). After the fact, focus groups can assist in determining what went right and what went wrong with a particular program, service, or product; the information can then be passed on to those in positions to follow-up and act on the data (e.g., ways to attract larger crowds to attend programs sponsored during next year's Black History Month).

ADVANTAGES OF FOCUS GROUPS

Both Krueger (1988) and Morgan (1988) identified many advantages of focus groups: (a) more appropriate for social science research when compared to some of the quantitative methods, (b) relatively easy to facilitate and conduct, (c) collection of information from group interaction, (d) an easily understood method producing believable information, (e) relatively inexpensive, (f) participation by a fairly large number of individuals, (g) an efficient use of time relative to amount of data collected, (h) able to be modified for use in a variety of settings, and (i) immediate testing of hypotheses in a group setting. As mentioned, focus groups involve "socially oriented research." Focus group members are informed ahead of time regarding their role in the research and are not treated as guinea pigs—being rewarded or punished dependent upon their "performance" in the experiment. As the name implies, focus groups involve groups of individuals interacting in relatively informal and comfortable settings, sharing opinions and perceptions on specified topics or areas determined ahead of time.

Focus groups are efficient. They allow the researcher to collect large amounts of data in relatively short periods of time. However, the inquirer should be careful not to overlook or cut short the amount of time that must be spent in developing and ordering the questions, training the facilitators and assistants, and conducting a trial focus group to ensure that everyone knows his or her role in the process and that the questions generate the kinds of data desired.

A time constraint is that planning time is needed for the preparation of thoughtful interview questions and the training of personnel. Although the primary goal in conducting the particular research or assessment activity is to collect data, a secondary goal when using other staff or students is to provide them with additional interpersonal and organizational skills. As student affairs professionals, we are always looking for ways to assist students in their own growth and development—for teachable moments—and involving them in this type of activity could do much for developing their interpersonal skills (e.g., putting people at ease, asking open-ended questions, being a team member in a research project). It may be important for the inquirer to set some priorities and parameters regarding the importance of the educational imperative as it relates to the goals of the study. How much time and energy does the inquirer want to invest in educating and training others in the use of focus groups as a means of soliciting and obtaining information?

Morgan (1988) noted that focus groups are well suited to topics that involve soliciting information regarding individuals' attitudes and cognition. Focus group interviews promote spontaneous responses from group members, and the format and setting usually allow those responses to be reconstructed and possibly altered as members listen to others' points of view. Focus groups are not as intimidating as one-on-one interviews. Other group members in a focus group provide some "insulation" so that an individual has time to think and ponder his or her initial responses. Facilitators should promote an environment within the focus group in which members can easily and readily change their minds without fearing an interrogation.

> Focus groups are neither as strong as participant observation on the naturalistic observation of interaction, nor as strong as interviewing on the direct probing of informant knowledge, but they do a better job of combining these two goals than either of the other two techniques. (Morgan & Spanish, 1984, p. 260)

DISADVANTAGES OR LIMITATIONS OF FOCUS GROUPS

When deciding upon the appropriate research methods to use, we also must explore fully any of the perceived or real limitations associated with the use of focus groups. No one method is free of problems, but if at all possible, it is important to be able to identify any disadvantages or limitations of a method *prior* to implementation. In so doing, the inquirer may be able to address these limitations by utilizing a particular method in conjunction with other methods (e.g., focus groups and individual interviews, individual interviews and participant observation, survey research and individual interviews coupled with document analysis). (See chapter 9 for a discussion on employing a variety of methods for the study and assessment of college students.)

When considering the use of focus groups, determine whether some of the known limitations will influence significantly the results of the particular study. A focus group facilitator does not have as much control over the direction of a group discussion as he or she has when conducting an individual interview. Data obtained from focus groups must be analyzed in relation to the group and the group discussion. It is critical that as the data are analyzed, the information is not taken out of the context in which it was discussed. The training of focus group facilitators and assistants takes time and practice. Becoming adept at asking open-ended questions and subtly redirecting the conversation back to the focus of the study takes practice. The composition and subsequent outcomes of focus groups may vary considerably; enough groups must be conducted to eliminate idiosyncrasies of a particular group. Finally, the logistics of preparing for and assembling focus groups can prove tedious.

READY, SET, GO

When using focus groups, it is easiest to divide the work into three phases: planning, conducting, and analyzing. After reading this section, the inquirer may choose to merge conducting focus groups and data analysis into one phase; but for the sake of clarity, conducting and analyzing are considered as two different phases here. Also discussed in this section are two elements that affect both planning and conducting successful focus groups: the skill level of the facilitator and the quality of the questions asked.

Planning

In planning any type of research activity, the inquirer must be able to articulate the purpose of the study and be able to define it to a degree of clarity and specificity to ensure that only one study is undertaken! This may sound elementary, but all too often a poorly designed study leads to growing problems and obstacles as the study progresses. Small flaws can be buried or overlooked at the outset but grow and become major problems as the inquirer begins to analyze data and draw conclusions. A problem statement that clearly defines the study is imperative. From there, the inquirer can begin to identify research methods most appropriate for conducting and completing the study.

Some practicalities involved in planning the project include resources available (e.g., financial, human, library, technical), time available, and institutional policies or procedures related to using human subjects. The majority of student affairs professionals are practitioners, and time is one of their scarcest resources. Therefore, it is critical that the soon-to-be inquirer be realistic when determining available resources to complete the project in a timely manner. Sometimes the less grandiose the plan, the more achievable the product.

Once the use of focus groups is determined to be appropriate for the study, many details must be addressed to ensure success. It is important to identify a "sample" at the outset: characteristics of the individuals who will comprise the different groups and a proposed number of groups to conduct. (Once the study progresses, the inquirer may decide to add or reduce the number of focus groups.) How will the inquirer or the focus group facilitator (they may be the same individual or two different individuals) contact individuals and entice them to attend the focus group? How much time is necessary to allocate for each focus group interview? How many members should be in each group? Where will the interviews be held to ensure comfort and convenience for members? What is the budget for the study? Has outside funding been sought? What is the time line (always plan for things to take longer than anticipated)? What kind of assistance will be needed from other individuals? Sticking to the time line and the budget are critical to the study's success. It is easier to make slight corrections or small adjustments before or during the focus group interviews rather than trying to resurrect an ambiguous and ill-conceived study after the fact.

The goals of the research will assist in determining the most appropriate number of focus groups and the size of each focus group. It is important to be realistic in the planning stages of the study; therefore, economics, the sensitive nature of the topic, and time should be factored into the equation for determining group size.

When it comes time to determine who should participate in the study, the inquirer naturally thinks about those individuals who can provide the most information. However, it is critical not to decide haphazardly and quickly upon a sample. Student affairs professionals are surrounded by students, and it may be all too easy to pick those closest who can be persuaded to volunteer their time. If only a narrow slice of the student population is selected to participate (e.g., student leaders, senior women, fraternity members), recognize and acknowledge that that is exactly what has happened. Morgan (1988) stressed how critical it is that focus group members feel comfortable and can talk with one another: "homogeneity in background, not homogeneity in attitudes" (p. 46). Gender, ethnicity, age, year in college, and "status" (e.g., social, academic major, living arrangement, financial) all are variables to consider as participant selections are made.

It may be helpful to tape record the discussions and transcribe the tapes. Using a tape recorder is one of the easiest ways to capture the data. An assistant is helpful in taking notes and recording who said what, but having the tapes transcribed into a written script can prove invaluable. If there is neither the time nor resources to have the tapes transcribed, it still can prove useful to listen to the tapes at a later date. It often takes all of the facilitator's concentration to keep the group on the topic and to keep the discussion moving in the desired direction. Memory often is best when recalling what one wants to hear rather than hearing the entire conversation and multiple meanings.

The inquirer may want to consider acting as the assistant in order to be able to pay more attention to the content and not to be so concerned with the process. Whatever role the inquirer decides to play, it is important that she or he sit down after the group interview and write field notes on what took place—noting especially poignant comments, any unusual group dynamics, or anything that emerged that should be included in the report or pursued with the next group. The assistant should take extensive notes throughout the group process, and this should be told to the group at the beginning of the meeting so as not to be overly distracting.

Setting the Stage

A crucial element in ensuring the success of focus groups is the skill level of the facilitator. Once again, the goals of the study affect the role of the facilitator. If the goal is one of exploring participants' attitudes and opinions, the facilitator may take a very low-key role, ask few questions, allow the discussion to follow its own course, and spend the majority of his or her time listening. If the study's goal is to reach closure on a particular topic or come up with specific action steps on an issue, the facilitator most likely will take a more active role in directing the discussion, following up on responses, moving the group along, and making adjustments as needed. Each style of facilitation brings with it advantages and disadvantages. It is the facilitator's responsibility to make a conscious and informed decision as to the appropriate style and tone to establish.

If a facilitator is not careful, she or he may become too involved in the discussion and group members may look to her or him for approval. A facilitator should avoid prolonged eye contact with any one member of the group and avoid adding personal comments related to the content of the discussion. A facilitator should be attentive to the group dynamics and attempt to "moderate" members who tend to dominate the discussion, solicit opinions from those members who are quieter or introverted, and keep all members on task and focused on the particular question being asked.

A facilitator's role can be made easier by laying out ground rules and group expectations at the beginning of each focus group. A facilitator may want to communicate some of the following expectations to participants:

1. Act in a way you respect. Do not behave or speak in a way that you might find offensive if the roles were reversed.
2. Take time to listen to others' comments. If you disagree with another's opinion, you will have time to give your point of view.
3. Feel free to ask questions of other focus group members. Ask them to clarify their comments if you do not understand the point they are trying to make.
4. It is important that you give examples when possible and provide details of your experiences and reasons for your opinions.
5. I am interested in hearing what you think, *not* what you think I want to hear. If I ask follow-up questions, it is for clarification and further articulation of your opinion. My questions are not intended to get you to change your mind.
6. You all have certain things in common, but your opinions and beliefs on a topic can be as different as night and day. There is no need to try to conform to what you think "others believe" or what you think "they want to hear."

Focus groups may appear to be self-directed and informal with conversations easily shifting from one topic to another without any forethought. If this, in fact, happens and the appropriate and necessary topics are being addressed, it is due most likely to the amount of planning on the part of all those involved in the study and the amount of skill on the part of the facilitator. The well-prepared inquirer conducts "trial" focus groups to test his or her questions, timing, and members' reactions.

Topic Selection

Interviewing and asking quality questions are skills that the facilitator must practice. A number of recent articles still cite *The Focused Interview* (1956), by Merton, Fiske, and Kendall, as one of the best resources for information on conducting effective focus groups. These authors noted that the inquirer sets the stage by defining the problem and determining the questions. The stage is predetermined, and the inquirer and facilitator turn their attention to considering the range of topics to explore, the level of desired specificity and depth, and the context from which options and beliefs come. Morgan's (1988) comment about the unique outcomes and results of conducting focus groups rings true especially for traditional age (18 to 24 years old) college students, who often are in the midst of defining their identities separate from parents or guardians.

> Without the interaction around a researcher-supplied topic, individuals are often safely unaware of their own perspective, and even when they do contemplate their world view, there is not the same effort needed to explain or defend it to someone who sees the world differently. (Morgan, 1988, p. 55)

As student affairs professionals, it may be more important at times to find the broadest possible perspective on a fairly general topic (e.g., first-year students' reactions to life at college, seniors' feelings of preparedness for entering the real world) rather than to focus on a narrowly defined topic. By developing more open-ended questions, facilitators may discover more and differing reactions (positive, negative, unintended) than they ever imagined and have a better chance of finding out "an exception, a deviation, an unusual interpretation [that] may suggest a revision, a reinterpretation, an extension, a new approach" (Dexter, 1970, p. 6).

Time to Begin

Conducting focus groups is similar to other social encounters, in which it is often best to begin with introductions, establishing rapport, and putting members at ease. The facilitator and assistant can do much to make individuals feel comfortable from the start by greeting each one individually and making small talk until others arrive. The facilitator may want to consider using name tags to assist in remembering names and for use in identifying who said what when it comes time to analyze the data.

Once focus group members have had a chance to gather, and the facilitator has taken care of any last minute details, it is time to begin the formal introductions and welcome, articulate the goals of the study, present any guidelines or group expectations, and provide an overview of what to expect and the proposed time frame for the discussion. This information should not be "new news" to anyone, but it is worth being repetitive to ensure that everyone has a mutual understanding of what is to come. Some institutions may require a human subject consent form that must be completed prior to the discussion.

It is finally time for the facilitator to pose the first question. The questions should move from general and nonthreatening to more specific. The intent should never be to ask threatening questions; however, it is important to realize that the more personal the question, the more threatening or intimidating it may appear to some members (especially in a group setting with peers).

Once information and opinions have been obtained from participants and the agenda has been covered, it is important to conclude the focus group as gracefully as it began. The facilitator or assistant may want to summarize the highlights of the discussion and solicit reactions, or members may be given one last opportunity to say anything still on their minds. "Is there anything else you would like to add to what's already been discussed?" "Do you feel that you've had an adequate chance to express your thoughts on the subject?" The facilitator should conclude by thanking them for their time and assistance in the study. If they are interested in the results, they should be informed how they can receive the final report.

Data Analysis

The inquirer may want to consider conducting focus groups and data analysis simultaneously to ensure greater clarity and specificity of information as the study proceeds. Many inquirers view data collection and data analysis as two different and sequential steps in conducting a research or assessment study. Whether data collection and data analysis are handled simultaneously or sequentially, the process should be outlined and documented prior to data collection. Conducting one focus group interview as a pilot study, analyzing the data, and using the information to make any modifications the inquirer deems necessary may be an ideal way to proceed.

Analyzing the huge amounts of data obtained from a qualitative study can appear to be an overwhelming task.

> The analysis process involves consideration of words, tone, context, non-verbal, internal consistency, specificity of responses, and big ideas. Data reduction strategies in the analysis are essential. Finally, and most important, analysis of focus group results must be systematic and verifiable. It is a careful and deliberate process of examining, categorizing, and tabulating evidence, and it is not hunches, guesses, or whatever one wants it to be. (Krueger, 1988, p. 119)

Reviewing the problem statement may sound ridiculous at this point in the game, but if well written, the problem statement can refocus the study back to its initial intent or original goals. Upon first reading, the data collected may appear to have nothing to do with the original purpose (e.g., the study wanted to identify why returning women students decided to go back for a college education, but the majority of the data focuses on the stresses and frustrations of being a single parent, maintaining a job, taking classes, and finding time to study). What does the inquirer do?

The constant comparative method (Glaser & Strauss, 1967) can be used to analyze any type of qualitative information and is intended to assist the inquirer in generating an integrated and plausible theory consistent with the data collected. Analyzing the data after each focus group will allow the inquirer to review and synthesize existing data and to consider more appropriate questions for gathering data from the next group.

The inquirer can begin to "unitize" data immediately after field notes are written or tapes transcribed. Units represent chunks of meaning. A unit could be as small as a single sentence or phrase, or as complex as a paragraph. Whatever its size, a unit must be able to stand alone and be understandable within the broad context of the study. Once data are broken into units, the inquirer can begin to "code" or categorize the data, which allows him or her to "cluster" the data around questions, themes, or hypotheses. Codes or categories can be descriptive, interpretive, or explanatory, ranging from the fairly concrete (e.g., number of students involved in extracurricular organizations) to the more inferential level of analysis (e.g., student leaders' perceptions of why other students do not get involved in extracurricular organizations) (Miles & Huberman, 1984).

Codes can be developed at different times throughout the collection and analysis of data. The inquirer may begin focus groups with a generic list of codes generated from the intent and underlying conceptual framework of the problem statement. These initial codes may be redefined, revised, or even discarded for different codes as the study proceeds and the inquirer talks and listens to more focus group discussions. The inquirer may start out with large numbers of categories or codes, and as data collection continues, themes may begin to emerge and smaller categories can be collapsed into broader, more overarching, defined themes.

Once the data have been analyzed, the inquirer must determine what is the most appropriate form to use to report the results. The report should (a) communicate the results of the study, (b) be organized in a logical manner (perhaps around themes developed from codes) for the intended audience to follow, and (c) document the time frame and history of the findings so people can pick up the report at a later date and have an understanding of the study (Krueger, 1988). Again, this decision must be made in the context of the problem statement: what the inquirer wanted to learn from the study, what was found, and who wanted to receive the results. Depending upon the audience and its expectations, the report may best be presented orally (e.g., to a student

affairs committee for the board of trustees, a student leadership conference, the student affairs staff) and followed up with an executive summary, written as a report and distributed, or written as a case study. The
possibilities are extensive.

CONCLUSION

Conducting focus group interviews is only one of the many ways to
collect information from and about students. However, it is an important
and potentially fruitful tool to consider when thinking about ways to
learn more about students and their needs. While conducting focus
groups, student affairs professionals are not only collecting data but also
spending quality time with students getting to know their needs and
interests, how they spend their time, and their views on a multitude of
topics. It can prove to be time well spent by all parties involved.

FURTHER READING

If more information on focus groups is desired, I strongly recommend
David L. Morgan's book, *Focus Groups as Qualitative Research* (1988), and
Richard A. Krueger's book, *Focus Groups: A Practical Guide for Applied
Research* (1988). Both books are easy to follow and very informative. (For
specific publication data, see the following reference list.) I challenge
readers to utilize focus groups on their campus and with their students.
Little has been written about the use or potential uses of focus groups
in higher education settings; it will be valuable for everyone in student
affairs to share such information with colleagues.

REFERENCES

Advertising Research Foundation. (1985). *Focus groups: Issues and approaches.*
New York: Author.
Bartos, R. (1986). Qualitative research: What it is and where it came from.
Journal of Advertising Research, 26(3), RC3-RC6.
Bellah, R. N., Madsen, R., Sullivan, W. M., Swidler, A., & Tipton, S. M. (1985).
Habits of the heart: Individualism and commitment in American life. New York:
Harper & Row.
Bellenger, D. N., Bernhardt, K. L., & Goldstrucker, J. L. (1979). Qualitative
research techniques: Focus group interviews. In J. B. Higginbotham & K. K.

Cox (Eds.), *Focus group interviews: A reader.* Chicago: American Marketing Association.

Blimling, G. S., & Miltenberger, L. J. (1984). *The resident assistant: Working with college students in residence halls.* Dubuque, IA: Kendall/Hunt.

de Tocqueville, A. (1969). In J. P. Mayer (Ed.), *Democracy in America* (G. Lawrence, Trans.). New York: Doubleday. (Original works published 1835 and 1840)

Dexter, L. A. (1970). *Elite and specialized interviewing.* Evanston, IL: Northwestern University Press.

Glaser, B. B., & Strauss, A. L. (·1967). *The discovery of grounded theory: Strategies for qualitative research.* Hawthorne, NY: Aldine de Gruyter.

Jacobi, M. (1991). Focus group research: A tool for the student affairs professional. *NASPA Journal, 28*(3), 195–201.

Krueger, R. A. (1988). *Focus groups: A practical guide for applied research.* Beverly Hills, CA: Sage.

Merton, R. K., Fiske, M., & Kendall, P. L. (1956). *The focused interview.* Glencoe, IL: Free Press.

Miles, M. B., & Huberman, A. M. (1984). *Innovation in education.* New York: Teachers College Press.

Morgan, D. L. (1988). *Focus groups as qualitative research.* Beverly Hills, CA: Sage.

Morgan, D. L., & Spanish, M. T. (1984). Focus groups: A new tool for qualitative research. *Qualitative Sociology, 7,* 253–270.

Rice, S. A. (Ed.). (1931). *Methods in social science.* Chicago: University of Chicago Press.

Russell, L. A. (1991). Assessing campus racism: The use of focus groups. *Journal of College Student Development, 32*(3), 271–272.

chapter 9

Triangulation: Intersecting Assessment and Research Methods

Ruth V. Russell
Frances K. Stage

Bill Frederick, dean of student affairs at Somerset College, is called to the office of President Katharine King, along with Virginia Skaggs, dean for academic affairs, and Alex Duffy, the college development officer.

President King has just returned from a meeting with the Board of Trustees concerned with declining enrollments (student headcount has continued to slip, to 1,856 this year from 2,138 5 years ago). The trustees want to determine whether they are meeting students' needs and to use a "value added" theme in their recruitment of new students. President King presented her plan for evaluation of assessment outcomes: measured growth in quantitative and verbal scores using formulas comparing incoming students' SAT or ACT scores with senior GRE scores. The trustees seemed about to approve the plan when Trustee Marguerite Smith raised an issue. The net result was that after an hour and a half of further discussion, Christopher Barrett, president of the board, demanded a broader assessment plan be presented at their next meeting, one going beyond additions to scores of verbal and quantitative skills.

Back in her office, the president, obviously under great stress, asks Dr. Frederick to meet with Trustee Barrett and her at the end of 3

123

months with a comprehensive assessment plan in hand. Although he does not know much about assessment, aside from a few articles he has read in journals, Dr. Frederick agrees provided that he be given access to resources of *all* campus offices; Dr. Skaggs and Dr. Duffy pledge their full support.

Situations such as the one just described occur with increasing frequency on today's college and university campuses. The research and assessment literature in education (as well as the other social sciences) is well known for disputes between proponents of various measurement methods. In a sense, these debates are a healthy sign; skepticism is an essential part of academic inquiry, and various methods represent important and critical perspectives on how best to find the truth and then how to describe what is found.

Equally important, however, is the concept of employing different information collection methods in an attempt to overcome validity problems that may be inherent in any one particular method (Brewer & Hunter, 1989). Regardless of which philosophical or epistemological perspective a researcher adopts, multiple sources of data collection can be used to optimize what is learned. As Patton (1980) observed, "Issues of methodology are issues of strategy, not of morals. Purity of method is no virtue" (p. 17). Dr. Frederick finds himself in agreement with this point of view, and his solution, which uses multiple sources, is described at the end of this chapter.

The strategy of implementing multiple methods is usually described as convergent methodology (Campbell & Fiske, 1959), multimethod/multitrait design (Campbell & Fiske, 1959), mixed-methods design (Greene & McClintock, 1985), convergent validation (Jick, 1979), or triangulation (Webb, Campbell, Schwartz, Sechrest, & Grove, 1981). Whatever the label, advocates of this approach share the conception that all methods (qualitative as well as quantitative) should be viewed as complementary rather than competing, and that triangulation will enhance or shed light on results.

The concept of employing multiple methods in a single study is not uncommon in the education literature (Cook, 1985; Cronbach, 1982; Fry, Chantavanich, & Chantavanich, 1981; Madey, 1982; Mark & Shotland, 1987; Mathison, 1988; Smith, 1986). Within student affairs and higher education, there are many examples of the multiple methods approach. It is employed most frequently in large research efforts involving teams of researchers who are studying an entire campus or even several campuses (e.g., Chickering, 1984; Fleming, 1985; Komorovsky, 1985; McClain & Krueger, 1985; Mentkowski & Loaker, 1985; Richardson & Bender, 1986). However, multiple approaches also have been applied in relatively small studies (Baxter-Magolda, 1990; Durst & Schaeffer, 1987; King, Wood, & Mines, 1990).

This chapter introduces readers to triangulation as a way of combining ideas from previous chapters to expand their own repertoires of research and assessment skills. Triangulation is described and an argument for its use is made. Further, the chapter proposes ways of interpreting triangulation results and discusses examples in higher education and student affairs literature. Finally, a continuation of the opening case study provides an illustration of triangulation in action.

WHAT IS METHOD TRIANGULATION?

In Denzin's (1978) pivotal discussion, four types of triangulation were outlined: data, investigator, theory, and method. *Data triangulation* refers simply to using several data sources, such as assessing more than one individual, or observing behavior at different times of day or year or in different settings. *Investigator triangulation*, also considered good practice, is the involvement of more than one investigator in the research process. *Theory triangulation* is more problematic and not unanimously endorsed. It proposes the possibility that results could be interpreted from more than one theoretical perspective.

> The great value of this strategy, as I see it, however, is its assurance that no study will be conducted in the absence of some theoretical perspective. In this sense it is most appropriate for the theoretically uncommitted, as well as for analysis of areas characterized by high theoretical incoherence. (Denzin, 1978, p. 307)

Finally, *method triangulation* is the most discussed type of triangulation and refers to the use of multiple methods in the study of a single phenomenon. This most common meaning of triangulation, method triangulation, is the type that is featured in this chapter.

For example, if we want to measure the degree of acceptance of cultural pluralism on campus, we could administer a cultural attitudes questionnaire, note student attendance at events devoted to others' cultures, conduct a series of focus group discussions on the topic with a wide range of students, examine institutional documents to determine enrollments in culturally focused college courses, or record reported incidents of cross-cultural harassment. If we use several of these methods in combination, we are employing method triangulation.

A college administrator who wants to determine the effectiveness of student leaders could interview the leaders themselves, unobtrusively observe their behavior at student organization meetings and events, conduct a content analysis of articles and editorials about the leaders in the student newspaper, and issue an opinion questionnaire about the leaders to other student samples.

Reasons for dropping out of college could be understood by interviewing students as they submit withdrawal forms at the registrar's office, sending parents of dropout students a questionnaire, giving dropout students a personality or attitude scale, interviewing former roommates of dropout students, and comparing the institutional records of dropout students with persisting students.

Method triangulation, however, is more complex than simply taking several measures on a subject of interest. The challenge lies in the interpretation of the results and the ways that information from all sources is used to describe and interpret findings. The researcher must actively seek points of intersection so that both mutually supportive results as well as seeming contradictions are fully discussed.

WHY GO TO ALL THIS TROUBLE?

As in geometry or in terrain surveying, multiple viewpoints allow for greater accuracy in describing the entire phenomenon. Other useful metaphors might be the detective's investigation of a crime, the approach of a car mechanic in troubleshooting the source of the engine rattle, or a physician's process of elimination for determining the location and/or name of an illness (Mathison, 1988).

Triangulation can capture a more complete, holistic, and contextual portrayal of the issue studied. It is here that the addition of qualitative methods to a quantitative assessment strategy or vice versa can play an especially prominent role by suggesting conclusions to which other methods will be blind (Jick, 1979). In a sense, triangulation may be most useful in enriching our understanding by allowing for new or deeper dimensions to be visible.

This was well demonstrated by Durst and Schaeffer (1987) in a study on the underlying factors of certain student problems. After several years of using questionnaires and formal interviews to study various aspects of student life, it became apparent to the investigators that additional methods needed to be incorporated into the project. The techniques chosen included using a graduate student from another college as a participant/observer for one semester, using voluntary student informants for one semester and giving them course credit for their participation, obtaining life histories of students, administering two surveys to a random sample of the entire student population, and administering a survey to a representative sample of the first-year class.

Initial analyses of the data in this study uncovered some aspects of the student culture that had been undiscovered through the former questionnaires and formal interviews design. For example, by adding qualitative research methods Durst and Schaeffer found that student friendship groups operated in many ways like kinship groups. Members of the friendship group were of both sexes (a typical finding from a questionnaire), but also dating was discouraged within the group unless both joined the group as part of an existing couple (revealed through the participant observations).

Method triangulation is typically perceived to be a strategy for improving the validity of research or assessment findings (Mathison, 1988). That is, "triangulation is supposed to support a finding by showing that independent measures of it agree with it or, at least, don't contradict it" (Miles & Huberman, 1984, p. 235). As demonstrated in the Durst and Schaeffer (1987) study, however, triangulation can also be a strategy for enriching conclusions by contributing new, explanatory findings. Viewing an issue or problem from various viewpoints exposes its many sides.

Further advocacy for this can be found by considering various ways of viewing the same phenomenon. That is, if the declining number of women's colleges is the sole criterion (Hirschorn, 1987), the conclusion might be that single-sex college education is failing. If, however, the success of graduates is the criterion (Rice & Hemmings, 1988), single-sex college education is succeeding. In another example, if changes in the percentage of academic degrees awarded to African-American students is the criterion (Albeiter, 1987), we conclude that we are slowly moving toward educational equity. However, if the percentage of African-American high school graduates who go on to college is the criterion (Albeiter, 1987), we are moving backward.

The point is that each narrow view can enhance the information collected and conclusions drawn. Alternative ways of measuring can serve to shed light on hidden issues not previously conceived of by administrators or researchers. The first result on educational equity for African-American students, examined alone, might lead the researcher to positive conclusions. In looking at two sources of data, the researcher learns that recruitment as well as retention of students is still a major problem. By adding a third component to the study, open-ended interviews of high school guidance counselors and college recruiters, further light would be shed on the phenomena.

THE UNDERLYING ASSUMPTION

Triangulation provides us with several important opportunities. It allows us to be more confident in our results. It can inspire the creative invention of methods—new ways of viewing a problem to balance with conventional methods. It may also help us to uncover a dimension of a phenomenon that is unremarkable within a more traditional approach. As a result, old theories may be refashioned or new theories developed. The use of multiple methods also often leads to a synthesis or integration of theories, a critical test for competing theories. Although all of these are eloquent and important rationales for triangulation, the real case must be made in terms of its underlying assumption.

The endorsement of method triangulation as a research strategy is based on a fundamental assumption about the "goodness" of findings: that bias inherent in a particular method can be canceled out and that the result will be convergence toward "reality." Mathison (1988) argued that bias inherent in any particular data collection method can be canceled out when used in conjunction with other methods. Triangulation seeks to enhance the assets and diminish the liabilities of a single method study. The effectiveness of triangulation rests on the premise that the weakness in each single method will be compensated by the counterbalancing strengths of another (see chapter 3; Jick, 1979; Terenzini, 1989).

Whereas a pretest-posttest research design risks such threats to internal validity as psychological or physical maturation or the effects of the test itself (Campbell & Stanley, 1963), time series analysis does not. Likewise, whereas a time series analysis risks such threats to internal validity as the plausibility of historical events explaining shifts found between time periods (Campbell & Stanley, 1963), other methods (e.g., a Solomon Four-Group design) do not.

Some (e.g., Shotland & Mark, 1987) have worried, however, about this assumption. Although it is intuitively sound to hope that using multiple methods to study a particular issue will balance out the bias in each individual method, what if, as is possible in the experimental examples just given, the methods are biased in the same way? This worry seems reasonable if little or inaccurate attention is paid to the initial selection and implementation of various methods. For example, an open format interview and a written response type of questionnaire are both likely to result in an underestimate of the use of alcohol by students during football games. However, counting (or weighing!) the beer cans that litter the stadium after games may be useful in balancing the bias. Therefore the administrator or researcher must deliberate carefully about the assessment or research questions asked in the study and the methods used to answer them.

If efforts are made to ensure that methods are used to cancel inherent biases, then what is left is more accurate knowledge about what is investigated. This means that when questioning is triangulated, answering will be more informed and more thorough.

WHAT'S AT THE END OF THE PATH?

In practice, triangulation as a strategy provides a rich and complex picture of the phenomenon studied, but rarely does it produce a clear, unambiguous path to a singular view. As presented by Mathison (1988), there are three possible outcomes from a study that employs multiple methods: convergence, inconsistency, and contradiction.

Convergence means that the data from various methods employed will provide evidence leading to a single proposition (Kidder & Fine, 1987). For example, student surveys, document analysis of student advocate office records, and interviews of campus counselors and advisers may yield a unified conclusion that sexual harassment exists on the campus. The likelihood of convergence is based, however, on the ability of the different methods to measure the same phenomenon. That is, if the investigators also chose to interview victims, results may provide a non-convergent view of campus sexual harassment. Victims may be reluctant to report thoroughly. Thus, while student surveys, official documents, and interviews of student affairs staff are measuring the incidence of sexual harassment, the victim interviews may be measuring something else: the experience of campus sexual harassment.

In a study by Jick (1979) on stress and anxiety, convergence was concluded when the archival, questionnaire, and interview data all agreed about the presence and source of anxiety. Yet, it is a delicate exercise to decide whether or not results have converged. In theory congruence is presumably easily apparent, but in practice there are few guidelines for systematically ordering eclectic data to determine corroboration. For example, should all data from a multimethod approach be weighted equally? Is all evidence equally useful? The determination is likely to be subjective.

A second and probably more commonly occurring outcome from a triangulated methods study is *inconsistency* among the results. When more than one method provides the data, a range of perspectives might not confirm a single conclusion. Rather, the evidence presents alternative conclusions. For example, a psychometric test given to first-generation college attenders may more strongly confirm the conclusion than does an interview with the students that locus of control influences adjustment to college.

An attempt to explain the inconsistency in these results requires going beyond the data obtained. By delving into the background of the data, by thoroughly understanding the context of the study, it is possible to construct a plausible explanation of inconsistent findings (Mathison, 1988). So in the above example of first-generation college attenders, locus of control may not have been as strongly supported by the interviews because of lack of expertise on the part of the interviewer or because the students themselves weren't able to verbalize such an elusive, psychological factor. Rather, the diverse data produced by the interviews help us to understand more fully that adjustment to college is a complex and many-factored issue that may include but also extends beyond a simple measure of locus of control.

A final possible outcome of triangulation is *contradiction.* It is possible not only for data to be inconsistent but also actually to be contradictory. Employing diverse methods can leave opposing views of the phenomenon studied. For example, in evaluating the quality of campus teaching, suppose we find an instructor whose aggregate evaluations on the standard campus instrument are consistently mediocre. However, this professor's classes are the first to fill and students continually ask for more sections of her classes.

Does this lead us to an incommensurable position? No. Contradiction of multiple-method-yielded results is appropriate to the goals of triangulation. Not only are convergent and inconsistent findings useful, but contradictory findings also may help us to understand the richness of what we are studying. Even contradictory findings provide more and better explanations. To complete the analysis of the professor's teaching, we seek explanation that accommodates the contradictory data.

In examining specific items on teaching evaluation results, we see that the teacher scores consistently high on items measuring enthusiasm, intellectual stimulation, and discussion. Her classroom scores on order and organization, consistency, and clarity of course assignments are low. An examination of the class syllabus reveals that a purpose of the course is to seek discrepant views from a set of assigned readings. Students are encouraged to bring such findings to class for group discussion. Dissonance, presentation of discrepant information, and open-ended assignments create an atmosphere conducive to learning (Stage, 1990), but such classroom characteristics do not fare well on standardized evaluation forms. In this case the unobtrusive measures were probably more accurate. Or further study into the context of the course's offering may reveal that the department has experienced an increase in the number of majors, and as this is a required course for majors, it automatically fills early because students worry it will be closed early. In this situation, the teaching evaluations may be more accurate.

SOME FOLKS ALREADY HAVE THEIR ACTS TOGETHER

Some researchers and administrators will recognize method triangulation as an approach that they have followed all along. However, for those who are just beginning to study in a particular area or who have discovered that multiple methodology has wider possibilities than options they are currently employing, we present some examples from the literature in higher education and student affairs. We are not attempting to be comprehensive here and hope that soon there will be many more examples to guide the design of college student assessment and research projects.

As mentioned earlier in this chapter, many of the prime examples of method triangulation were conducted by teams of researchers who had many resources and examined entire campuses or several campuses. Although many of the readers of this book are not envisioning such large undertakings, perusing one or more of these volumes might prove enlightening. They serve as excellent examples of the variation of data collection and interpretation possible.

Probably the best known of the examples cited here is Chickering's work from the late 1960s (Chickering, 1984) on college student development. The project involved a study of institutional characteristics, student characteristics, attrition, and development in 13 small colleges. Researchers employed a battery of questionnaires juxtaposed with intensive interviews to study the college student experience. The result was one of the most widely cited theories in student affairs.

In a landmark study of African-American students, Fleming (1985) collected data from over 1,000 students at seven colleges. The purpose was to compare these students' experiences at predominantly Black and at predominantly White institutions. Fleming employed a broad range of quantitative measures supplemented by personal interviews, resulting in the most comprehensive understanding yet of the African-American college student experience.

In a study focused on women's identities on a single campus, Komorovsky (1985) combined data from 232 sets of scales, intensive interviews, and diaries. On the value of combining qualitative and quantitative data Komorovsky stated that without qualitative data:

> A statistical correlation that is a mere accident of sampling would not be supported by such further evidence. For example, we found an

association between strained parental marriages (or divorce) on the one hand and the daughter's career commitment on the other. . . . supporting evidence for this association was forthcoming in several interviews . . . daughters of divorced parents often attributed their determination to pursue a career to the failure of their mothers' traditional role. (p. 9)

Throughout the book, quotations from interviews and diaries added depth and explication to the findings. In another study, Richardson and Bender (1986) focused on colleges that were successful in promoting achievement of minority students. Data from surveys of graduates, open-ended interviews, and site visits were combined to develop case studies for each of 10 institutions.

McClain and Krueger (1985) described a value-added student assessment model that employed multiple methods. Standard institutional demographic data, ability and achievement measures from national standardized tests, and questionnaires administered at freshman orientation, during the undergraduate years, for graduating seniors, and alumni were used. The data collected were combined to devise ways of improving student learning and development throughout the curriculum.

A multifaceted assessment process that followed the development of each student at a small liberal arts college for women was described by Mentkowski and Loaker (1985). The assessment focused on communication, analysis, problem solving, valuing, social interaction, environmental responsibility, world involvement, and aesthetic response. Assessments by instructors, off-campus assessors, peers, and the students were employed. The researchers combined traditional quantitative measures, standardized subject-specific instruments developed by faculty, and in-depth interviews to provide a broad picture of student growth.

Several less well-known but important studies also employ method triangulation. These tend to focus on a particular setting within a college campus or on a particular aspect of student growth or development. They are more likely to serve as examples of the kinds of research or assessments most readers have the resources to assemble.

Baxter-Magolda (1990) combined a written instrument and open-ended interviewing to assess college students' epistemological development. Themes generated from the interviews were used to corroborate quantitative findings. In a study by King, Wood, and Mines (1990), standardized test scores were combined with two questionnaires—the Watson-Glazer Critical Thinking Appraisal and the Cornell Critical Thinking Test—and the Reflective Judgment Interview to examine undergraduate and graduate students' critical thinking skills.

Munoz (1986) combined structured interviews, a demographic questionnaire, and the College Environment Stress Index to study Hispanic college students' stress. Researchers concluded that these students need more encouragement to use campus support systems and that researchers as well as educators need greater awareness of these students' problems.

Perhaps the finished products just described still leave some wondering how mixing methods can be useful on their own campuses. The continuation of the case study from the beginning of the chapter, presenting a model of a small liberal arts campus's approach to outcomes assessment that employs a multiple methods approach, will help to clarify.

TRIANGULATION IN ACTION: DR. FREDERICK'S SOLUTION

Back in his own office, Dr. Frederick begins by reading the statement of the mission and goals of the institution. From that he finds four themes for the assessment: leadership development, critical thinking, global citizenship, and problem solving through technology. He next forms a *focus group* of various department chairs. They are asked to discuss a series of questions relevant to the four themes: What should graduates of Somerset have in common? How do you know when you've succeeded in educating a student in your major? Finally, Dr. Frederick calls several alumni and asks them "What do you look for in a new professional?"

From these lists, Dr. Frederick generates ideas for a variety of measures surrounding each theme that could be obtained from the major campus divisions. He recruits the aid of the academic affairs office in obtaining incoming students' SAT or ACT scores in comparison with graduating students' GRE scores. For the assessment plan the English faculty agree to develop a protocol for assessment of writing skills through students' senior projects, for comparison with their routinely conducted assessments of students' first-year English papers. Senior projects will also be used to assess word processing and/or statistical package usage skills. Additionally, *existing documents*, such as enrollments in senior topical seminars on global issues, will be recorded. Participation in theatre and musical productions, student publications, and art shows will be recorded. Finally, numbers of students applying and being accepted to graduate schools will be recorded by department.

Resources from the development office will be used to generate information about the success of graduates from alumni records. A leadership development program that matches students with community leaders will be assessed with a *survey instrument* of community leaders. The plan also calls for student participants to take a leadership skills

	Academic Affairs	Student Affairs	Development/Alumni
Leadership development	Musical and theatre productions Graduate school acceptances Focus groups	Participation and leadership in campus events Case studies of campus leaders	Community Leaders Program assessment Volunteerism in community organizations Tracking of alumni employment Historical profiles
Critical thinking	Writing skills SAT growth comparison Student publications Art shows Senior projects Focus groups	Case studies	Historical profiles
Global citizenship	Senior seminars Enrollments Focus groups	Participation in specific campus events Case studies	Volunteerism in community organizations Historical profiles
Problem solving with technology	Senior projects Writing skills Focus groups	Case studies	Tracking of graduates' employment Historical profiles

FIGURE 1
Measures by Themes Within Campus Divisions

test at the beginning and the end of the year. Numbers of undergraduates volunteering for service in community organizations also will be recorded. Additionally, graduating students' employment and subsequent job patterns will be tracked. Finally, a *historical analysis* of a series of profiles from the alumni magazine will be conducted.

Dr. Frederick's own division, student affairs, in addition to overseeing the assessment, commits to putting together *case studies* of four students: a national merit scholarship winner, a first-generation attender, an ethnic minority student, and a special admit "borderline student." The division will also provide routinely recorded *nonreactive documentation* of attendance at cultural, world issue, human rights, political, and environmental demonstrations and events.

In order to facilitate planning as well as triangulating the data gathered, Frederick creates a matrix (Figure 1) containing measures by each campus office broken down by theme. In using the chart, those involved in the project can see weak areas in measurement of themes as well as pieces of data to be analyzed in concert for full assessment of a given theme.

Dr. Frederick's plan is presented and approved at the next board meeting.

CONCLUSION

Although this case study is obviously hypothetical, it is not too idealistic. The solution to Somerset's assessment crisis involves using resources and gathering information that are easily available on most college campuses. No special funds are used to bring in an outside evaluation team. Aside from covering the costs of GRE examinations for *all* graduating seniors, existing campus resources are used to examine the outcomes that the campus promises its students. Finally, using multiple methods enables the administrators to give a richer, fuller assessment of value added.

The moral of this story is that the whole is greater than the sum of its parts (Smith, 1986). In this chapter the case is made for triangulation, for combining diverse data collection methods in college student research and assessment. The objections are well known. Triangulation costs too much, pits philosophical paradigms against each other, requires skills that are beyond most individuals and investigation teams, leaves too much freedom in drawing conclusions, and so on. Nevertheless, the merits outweigh the objections.

College and university campuses are routinely faced with diversity and contradiction. We can rarely take data about college students and the college environment at face value. It has been learned through experience, as well, that the often-mentioned duck test of knowledge (if it looks like a duck, walks like a duck, and quacks like a duck, then it is a duck) is all too rarely applied.

The fact of the matter is that research and assessment findings are determined both by the reality we seek to comprehend and by the patterns of thought and behavior involved in the act of inquiry itself. Because various methods of inquiry involve different patterns of thought and behavior, they may generate very different patterns of results. This can be discouraging and frustrating to beginners with high hopes. However, a great benefit of method triangulation is that it teaches both humility and confidence (Brewer & Hunter, 1989). We can admit to the chance of error and misinterpretation, but we can also assert that without triangulation there is little chance for truth.

FURTHER READING

We recommend two additional resources for further reading and explanation. First, *Multiple Methods in Program Evaluation* edited by M. M. Mark and R. L. Shotland, and published in 1987 by Jossey-Bass in the New Directions for Program Evaluation series, is useful in exploring a diverse set of topics germane to the use of multiple methods. Second, *Multimethod Research: A Synthesis of Styles* by J. Brewer and A. Hunter provides a thorough discussion of many uses of triangulation. It was published by Sage in 1989.

REFERENCES

Albeiter, S. (1987). Black enrollments: The case of the missing students. *Change, 19*(3), 14–19.

Baxter-Magolda, M. B. (1990). The impact of freshman year on epistemological development: Gender differences. *Review of Higher Education, 13*(3), 249–258.

Brewer, J., & Hunter, A. (1989). *Multimethod research: A synthesis of styles.* Beverly Hills, CA: Sage.

Campbell, D. T., & Fiske, D. W. (1959). Convergent and discriminant validation by the multitrait-multimethod matrix. *Psychological Bulletin, 56*, 81–105.

Campbell, D. T., & Stanley, J. C. (1963). *Experimental and quasi-experimental designs for research.* Boston: Houghton Mifflin.

Chickering, A. W. (1984). *Education and identity.* San Francisco: Jossey-Bass.

Cook, T. D. (1985). Postpositivist critical multiplism. In R. L. Shotland & M. M. Mark (Eds.), *Social science and social policy.* Newbury Park, CA: Sage.

Cronbach, L. J. (1982). *Designing evaluations of educational and social programs.* San Francisco: Jossey-Bass.

Denzin, N. K. (1978). *The research act: A theoretical introduction to sociological methods.* New York: McGraw-Hill.

Durst, M., & Schaeffer, E. M. (1987). Using multimethod research techniques to study college culture. *Journal of the National Association for Women Deans, Administrators, and Counselors, 51*(1), 22–26.

Fleming, J. (1985). *Blacks in college: A comparative study of student success in Black and in White institutions.* San Francisco: Jossey-Bass.

Fry, G., Chantavanich, S., & Chantavanich, A. (1981). Merging quantitative and qualitative research techniques: Toward a new research paradigm. *Anthropology and Education Quarterly, 12*(2), 145–158.

Greene, J., & McClintock, C. (1985). Triangulation in evaluation: Design and analysis issues. *Evaluation Review, 9*(5), 523–545.

Hirschorn, M. W. (1987). Plan to admit men to Wheaton College stirs bitter fight on and off the campus. *Chronicle of Higher Education, 33*(36), 30–34.

Jick, T. D. (1979). *Process and impacts of a merger: Individual and organizational perspectives.* Unpublished doctoral dissertation, New York State School of Industrial and Labor Relations, Cornell University.

Kidder, L. H., & Fine, M. (1987). Qualitative and quantitative methods: When stories converge. In M. M. Mark and R. L. Shotland (Eds.), *Multiple methods in program evaluation* (New Directions for Program Evaluation, No. 35). San Francisco: Jossey-Bass.

King, P. M., Wood, P. K., & Mines, R. A. (1990). Critical thinking among college and graduate students. *Review of Higher Education, 13,* 167–186.

Komorovsky, M. (1985). *Women in college: Shaping new feminine identities.* New York: Basic Books.

Madey, D. L. (1982). Some benefits of integrating qualitative and quantitative methods in program evaluation, with illustrations. *Educational Evaluation and Policy Analysis, 4,* 223–236.

Mark, M. M., & Shotland, R. L. (Eds.). (1987). *Multiple methods in program evaluation* (New Directions for Program Evaluation, No. 35). San Francisco: Jossey-Bass.

Mathison, S. (1988). Why triangulate? *Educational Researcher, 17*(2), 13–17.

McClain, C. J., & Krueger, D. W. (1985). Using outcomes assessment: A case study in institutional change. In P. Ewell (Ed.), *Assessing educational outcomes* (New Directions for Institutional Research, No. 47). San Francisco: Jossey-Bass.

Mentkowski, M., & Loacker, G. (1985). Assessing and validating the outcomes of college. In P. Ewell (Ed.), *Assessing educational outcomes* (New Directions for Institutional Research, No. 47). San Francisco: Jossey-Bass.

Miles, M. B., & Huberman, A. M. (1984). *Qualitative data analysis: A sourcebook of new methods.* Beverly Hills, CA: Sage.

Munoz, D. (1986). Identifying areas of stress for Chicano undergraduates. In M. Olivas (Ed.), *Latino college students.* New York: Teachers College Press.

Patton, M. Q. (1980). *Qualitative evaluation methods.* Beverly Hills, CA: Sage.

Rice, J. K., & Hemmings, A. (1988). Women's colleges and women achievers: An update. *Signs, 13*(3), 546–559.

Richardson, R. C., & Bender, L. W. (1986). *Helping minorities achieve degrees: The urban connection. A report to the Ford Foundation.* New York: Ford Foundation. (EDRS #ED277436)

Shotland, R. L., & Mark, M. M. (1987). Improving inferences from multiple methods. In M. M. Mark & R. L. Shotland (Eds.), *Multiple methods in program evaluation* (New Directions for Program Evaluation, No. 35). San Francisco: Jossey-Bass.

Smith, M. L. (1986). The whole is greater: Combining qualitative and quantitative approaches in evaluation studies. In D. D. Williams (Ed.), *Naturalistic evaluation* (New Directions for Program Evaluation, No. 30). San Francisco: Jossey-Bass.

Stage, F. K. (1990). Research on college students: Commonality, difference, and direction. *Review of Higher Education, 13*, 249–258.

Terenzini, P. T. (1989). Assessment with open eyes: Pitfalls in studying student outcomes. *Journal of Higher Education, 60*, 644–664.

Webb, E. K., Campbell, D. T., Schwartz, L., Sechrest, L., & Grove, J. B. (1981). *Nonreactive measures in the social sciences.* Boston: Houghton Mifflin.

chapter 10

Toward Research Evolution

Frances K. Stage

A s we move toward the next millennium we will see techniques for conducting research on college and university students that are increasingly diverse. Those who study college and university students have discovered that many of their most burning questions cannot be answered through traditional methods (the survey, structured interview, and standardized instrument).

Similarly, with the development of the assessment movement has come an attendant dissatisfaction with traditional measures of student growth and development in college. There is a need for administrators, researchers, and professionals to understand the alternatives that exist for the collection of data on the college student experience. Additionally, there is a need for consumers of such information to discern high-quality research and assessment.

Some scholars have advocated that researchers move from a probabilistic view of the world toward a view of future possibilities. A researcher with such a view, a "critical theorist," asks questions that will shape society in the future. How can we encourage students to adopt a sense of responsibility toward others? Can students learn to place greater value on developing a meaningful philosophy of life rather than on more mercenary goals? How can we encourage the development of members of historically underrepresented populations? Only when college student theorists and researchers ask such questions can the answers help create a more positive world rather than merely describe its imperfections.

In the last 15 years we have learned many new lessons about educating college and university students. One of the most important is that we can no longer be satisfied with courses, services, and programs geared toward the mythical "average college student." We now know that that student is increasingly rare. In the late 1970s enrollment forecasters were predicting steep declines in college enrollments through the end of this century. After the baby boom had expanded the higher education infrastructure of the United States, declines in the population threatened many colleges and universities.

This decline in numbers of average college students was filled with diverse students whom we sought to enroll at our institutions. We enjoined them to come with promises of educational fulfillment. We rejoiced in our swelling enrollment figures in the face of predictions of decline. Amid the rejoicing, however, we noticed problems. We were ill equipped to provide the education we had promised. Many new students fled our hallowed institutions nearly as quickly as they had come.

Today, with our new populations of students, with the exciting range of experiences, abilities, and talents on campus, we ask age-old questions again. Who are these college students? How can we provide comfortable climates for all students to live and learn? How can we enable each student to develop to his or her full potential? We hope that this book begins to explain new ways of asking these old questions.

As consumers of research on college students, student affairs staff are in a position of guiding research practices. When we continue to question and express dissatisfaction with research that provides only limited answers to short-sighted questions change will result. Questions must be asked in ways that seek answers not just from the majority or the average student but from individuals on our campuses as well.